26.6.07

Joseph Conrad

Joseph Conrad

RUTH L. NADELHAFT

Professor of English
University of Maine

HUMANITIES PRESS INTERNATIONAL, INC.
Atlantic Highlands, NJ

First published 1991 in the United States of America by
HUMANITIES PRESS INTERNATIONAL, INC.,
Atlantic Highlands, NJ 07716

Library of Congress Cataloging-in-Publication Data

Nadelhaft, Ruth L. *1938–*
    Joseph Conrad / Ruth L. Nadelhaft.
        p. cm. – (Feminist readings)
    Includes bibliographical references.
    ISBN 0–391–03721–8 – ISBN 0–391–03722–6 (pbk.)
    1. Conrad, Joseph. 1857–1924–Political and social views.
2. Feminism and literature–Great Britain–History–20th century.
3. Sex role in literature. 4. Women in literature. I. Title.
II. Series.
PR6005.04Z78437 1991
823'.912–dc20   90–25782
                                                                              CIP

Printed in Great Britain

For Jerry
and the memory of Paul L. Wiley

Feminist Readings

The *Feminist Readings* series has been designed to investigate the link between literary writing and feminist reading by surveying the key works of English Literature by male authors from new feminist perspectives. Working from a position which accepts that the notion of gender difference embraces interrelationship and reciprocity as well as opposition, each contributor to the series takes on the challenge of reassessing the problems inherent in confronting a 'phallocentric' literary canon, by investigating the processes involved in the translation of gender difference into the themes and structures of the literary text.

Each volume surveys briefly the development of feminist literary criticism and the broader questions of feminism which have been brought to bear on this practice, from the initial identification of 'phallocentrism', through the tendency of early feminist critics to read literature as a sociological document, through to feminist criticism's current capacity to realign the discoveries of a wide range of disciplines in order to reassess theories of gender difference. The tendency of the feminist critic to privilege texts written by women and the notion that it might be possible to identify an autonomous tradition of 'women's writing' can offer a range of challenges to current feminist criticism, and the key texts by male authors surveyed by the series are considered in this light.

Can there be a politics of feminist criticism? How might a

theory of sexual difference be seen to be directly applicable to critical practice? The series as a whole represents a comprehensive survey of the development by various theories of gender difference, and, by assessing their applicability to the writing of the most influential male writers of the literary tradition, offers a broadly revisionary interpretation of feminist critical practice.

Contents

Acknowledgements

The Humanities Division of the University of Maine, overworked, underpaid, and undervalued, has been for years the most supportive environment in the university for adventurers in feminist thought, practice and friendship. I appreciate the enthusiastic encouragement of my colleagues and friends in the Division. My children, Erica and Matthew, scholars themselves, have been interested and encouraging; their standards for themselves have reminded me of the continuing power of academic work, the value of thinking and writing out of conviction and desire. I also appreciate the interest of my parents, Albert and Esther Levy, who are delighted to have lived long enough to see this manuscript finished. Laurie House, a student in the Honors Program, became my Merit work study student and accumulated notes for me about the Conrads' domestic lives and the attitudes of critics to that relationship.

This book is for my husband, Jerry, whose love and companionship are bedrock for me always. It is also for the memory of Paul Wiley, whose presence at the University of Wisconsin had everything to do with my decision to stay in graduate school and try to do meaningful work.

Introduction

What would happen if one woman told the truth about her life?
The world would split open.
                        Muriel Rukeyser, 'Käthe Kollwitz',
                    from *The Speed of Darkness* (Bogan, 1974)

A feminist reading of the works of Joseph Conrad needs a good deal of introduction for three different, but interrelated, reasons. First of all, Conrad was for almost all of his writing life regarded as a writer of literature for men. Though he desired popularity and general acceptance, he did not receive it until the publication of *Chance*, in 1913, a novel which many of his critics took as pandering to an audience interested more in romance than in serious literature. The nature of Conradian criticism for many years created around his life and work an atmosphere peculiarly masculine. A second reason for extended introduction has to do with the nature of feminist criticism itself, which is now very diverse but which generally does not allow for much critical approval of male authors as they choose to portray female characters. And finally, a feminist reading of Joseph Conrad is designed in large part to reclaim Conrad for women readers for whom he has been almost a clandestine pleasure, in the face of the male critical hierarchy and feminist disapproval. Accomplishing that reclamation involves some new and different accounts of what a feminist reading means in relation to the work of Joseph Conrad. Attention

1

to many texts though not all, including all the major works, will reveal the pleasures, particularly for the woman reader, of a novelist who escapes categorisation if he is read from this new perspective now available, with additional biographical information, to supply the grounding for powerful and authentic women characters who speak in recognisable accents to a new generation of readers.

Critical interest in Conrad had always been strong: from the beginning of his career, when the publisher's reader, Edward Garnett, recognised the powerful appeal of *Almayer's Folly*, influential male critics have always recognised Conrad as 'one of us', a novelist of virility and strength with a capacity for focusing on issues of major importance: imperialism, colonialism, corruption. By now, three generations of such critics have made Conrad the centre of what almost amounts to a critical industry. Biographies emerge at intervals, some directed primarily towards illumination of his life, some integrating his life and his works, some firmly focused on the works themselves. So large is the body of work, and the interest in it, that a current Conradian project, by Ian Watt, takes an entire volume of many pages to bring Conrad's life and work only to the end of the nineteenth century.

With few exceptions, critics who write about Conrad have been male. The major biographies, by Jocelyn Baines and Albert Guerard, and the critical biographies by Frederick R. Karl and Ian Watt have all been written by men. A few women have written about Conrad, such as M. C. Bradbrook, Eloise Knapp Hay, and Claire Rosenfield, but the prevailing interest in and appropriation of Conrad have from the beginning of his career been male. In itself, that preponderance of male ownership is not surprising, since men have made up most of the army of critics for generations. But there has been a particular slant to the male ownership of Conrad which has worked to defeat any likelihood of female interest developing. Although from his earliest novels Conrad created and developed powerful and credible images of women, male friends, colleagues, and critics disregarded those images and focused instead on images of men: male uses of power and the passage from illusion to disillusion.

Later, in the 1960s, when criticism became explicitly psychoanalytical, another Conrad biographer, Bernard C. Meyer, developed a view of Conrad which used incomplete biographical information about Conrad's early childhood to serve as the foundation for a theory about Conrad which further discouraged female interest or identification with the novelist or his characters. Meyer described Conrad as deeply frightened by women, inclined through the early loss of his mother to project on to women terrifying powers of destructiveness and abandonment. Deeply invested in his theoretical approach, Meyer offered critical readings which regularly emphasised the 'monstrous' and frightening aspects of women characters. Especially in the early novels, which contain portraits of Malaysian and mixed race women, Meyer saw Conrad expressing fear and distrust of women's sexually devouring natures. As Meyer describes his approach, he makes his analysis clear in its most restrictive form:

> Conrad's heroes are motherless wanderers, postponing through momentary bursts of action their long-awaited return to a mother, whose untimely death has sown the seeds of longing and remorse, and whose voice, whispered from beyond the grave, utters her insistent claim upon her son's return.[1]

Meyer attributes to Conrad guilt for his mother's physical decline in their shared exile, suggesting that 'unencumbered by the care of a small and sick child, Evelina might have better endured the arduous hardships which had befallen her'.[2] Fear and guilt thus become for Meyer the twin characteristics of women for Conrad, and he attaches to women characters either the attributes of the failing mother or the devouring and murderous lover. To further his interpretation, Meyer regularly takes the accusations of male characters about women for Conrad's own. Meyer represents perhaps the most vivid example of the critical approach to Conrad which has regularly blurred the important distinction between the author and the text. Key women characters who articulate female and even feminist criticism of the patriarchal world of the Conradian protagonist are thus dismissed as devouring, mad, possessive, and venomous, as though the characterisations come directly from the author.

Although there have always been critics more interested in Conrad's political insights than in his development of character, the conjunction of interests represented by Conrad's many male critics led to a complex and perhaps inevitable intersection of misreadings. Conrad found himself during his lifetime denied the popularity he craved for both financial and emotional reasons, at least in part because of the critical atmosphere surrounding his books. Each new production was welcomed as further confirmation of the Conradian image: 'great' literature illuminating the troubled souls of male protagonists engaged in public quests for meaning in lives devoid of women.

When critics discussed Conrad's women characters, as indeed when they discussed the women in his life, they described either weak, sentimental, and fragile women or they attributed a failure of intellectual or political acumen to those women who remained central to his life and works. Generations of critics have puzzled over the long and apparently companionable marriage between Joseph and Jessie Conrad; the disparity in age and background puzzled and even irritated many critics and critical friends who resorted to complex and demeaning formulations to explain away the enduring fact of a successful relationship. Frederick R. Karl, an influential critic, took issue with some of Meyer's speculations about the oddities of Conrad's marriage. He disagreed with Meyer's attribution of failure to the marriage based on Conrad's psychological incapacity for marriage; instead, Karl offered a scarcely less demeaning explanation. He writes:

> I prefer to view Conrad's marriage as really a means toward his major and dominant preoccupation: *to establish the best terms on which he could continue as an author.*[3]

A territorial claim to the life and work of Conrad thus resulted in a tacit critical agreement about the meaning and place of women and the feminine in Conrad's life and work.

That place and meaning need better understanding, which is now possible. Further translations of familial letters and materials have brought to light additional background information which locates the sources of Conrad's experience in a marriage between his parents, and an early childhood, which were not simply the tragic emotional desert regularly portrayed by earlier critics. The dead mother, taken by psychoanalytical critics, readers and biographers as the simple source of imagery of abandonment and terror, emerges from the new material in a different guise.

Familial letters translated, compiled and edited by Zdzislaw Najder provide a glimpse of the relationship between Conrad's parents which suggests that the strong woman need not take the stereotypical form ascribed to her by psychoanalytical critics such as Meyer and then accepted by other critics whose interpretations benefited from such assumptions.

In the Introduction to his *Conrad under Familial Eyes*, Najder points out that no psychoanalytic critic of Conrad's work had access to an adequate amount or type of material. 'To formulate a biographical theory plausible within the framework of psychoanalysis, one ought to study the pertinent facts no less carefully than one has studied Freud.' Najder goes on to note what may still be the critical point regarding the characters of Conrad's parents:

> Even if what Conrad wrote about his parents were liable to only one interpretation, still we could not know what his relations with them might have been if we did not know what kind of people they were. It is not a matter of indifference whether Conrad's father was really a brooding, humourless fanatic, and his mother a 'cold' and 'austere' person (as some biographers imagine), or not. Making their letters available should at least put a stop to such irreponsibly fantastic statements.[4]

Najder focuses, as well he might, on the counter-factual way in which Conradian critics have constructed a biography and a psychology for Conrad based on inadequate familiarity with sources. He does not focus on the inadequacy of Freudian psychology itself as a means to full understanding of Conrad and his attitudes towards women in his life and in his work. It remained for feminist criticism, in a variety of fields, to provide powerful explanations of the problems with Freudian formulations as a basis for personal or literary understanding. Through Najder's work we are now able to encounter the figure of Conrad's mother unencumbered by filtered Freudianism, and her image and her example may be read in a positive, empowering way, instead of the negative and demoralising way depicted by Meyer and other biographers. Rather, the genesis of such powerful figures as Emilia Gould and Natalia Haldin, as well as the equally powerful but misread figures of Nina Almayer and Aissa, lies in the figure of Ewa Korzeniowska. The letters from Ewa to Apollo Korzeniowski illustrate the integration of public and private concerns into a life of affection, power and grace.

Feminist literary criticism, in its many facets, allows for a new integration of the biographical and the literary, both by the author and by the reader. It is this aspect of feminist criticism, rather than some of its other varieties, which will be particularly helpful in a reading of the life and works of Joseph Conrad. 'Literary criticism has both to ask: what is sexual difference and (simultaneously) how is sexual difference intervening in the act of reading? It has to define difference while trying to find it out.'[5]

In its earliest modern form, feminist criticism properly focused on the rediscovery and the reclaiming of women's literary history. 'Gynocriticism', as Elaine Showalter called it in a moment of desperate playfulness, was a necessary and legitimate first focus. The rediscovery of published, unpublished, and lost work led, with powerful logic, to the rethinking of genre, the way in which judgements about form itself had governed the attribution of value to the written word. Feminine 'forms' received scrutiny and validation; the role of criticism necessarily became more complex as the critic encountered new sorts of literature which seemed often to bypass the critic in their immediacy and directness.

At the same time, another aspect of contemporary feminist criticism emerged, a highly technical theoretical form of criticism which turned attention to the nature of language itself and the ways in which language creates gender along with sensibility. This aspect of feminist literary criticism is vital to the development and understanding of contemporary readers, in its account of the ways in which women have been systematically denied access to the primal sources of language as a masculine activity; it suggests a number of responses on the theoretical level, and it certainly requires radical rewriting of the acts of speaking and writing. New understanding of the ways in which female semiotics precedes formal language promises to restore, at least at the level of theory, a direct access to the sources of creativity for women at a level beneath and beside the formal and formerly authoritative level of male creativity and criticism.

However, these powerful theoretical modes of feminist criticism suggest the relinquishment of much of what has, in fact, been written and read by male authors. As Maggie Humm remarks during her discussion of language and psychoanalysis in *Feminist Criticism*, 'It is tempting not to ask the obvious questions. If "the woman" is absent in male discourse, how can she speak in books? Who is speaking, and who is asserting the Otherness of woman? If woman's silence and absence constitutes her feminism, how can she ever speak in the name of women?'[6] There has been a general assumption, challenged only occasionally, as by Nina Auerbach, which suggests that it is not possible for women, as characters or as readers, to be accurately represented in the works of men. Unless the feminist critic uses some of the powerful critical tools of the past, including such traditional modes as biography, along with close reading which assumes that there is 'a text' which can be 'read' by a reader, some of the valuable aspects of an author such as Joseph Conrad must become even more inaccessible, ironically not at the hands of the male critical industry that initially claimed him, but through the aegis of powerful lines of enquiry developed by important feminist critics. A sense of the personal and political history against which Conrad's texts emerged rescues the voices of the many women characters who speak strongly against the patri-archal culture which both welcomed and subtly rejected Conrad as a man and as a writer.

A contemporary feminist critic such as Gayatri Spivak

combines some of the most sophisticated techniques of deconstruction with a sharp interest in Marxism and the colonial present. A new feminist reading of Conrad must take into account the nature of imperialism, of course, but it must also acknowledge the degree to which the women who were objectified by imperialism come to their subjectivity in the literature Conrad created around them. In reading through his life to his text, and through the text to the characterisations, the contemporary feminist reader is able to hear more directly from the women than were his critics and readers in earlier times. Critics who were themselves more shaped by the values and the value systems of imperialism and patriarchy read into the women characters their fears and their loyalties, attributing them to the author as a matter of course.

At the same time that the new feminist reader benefits from an understanding of the ways in which Conrad was appropriated by the patriarchal critical world which formed the very subject about which he wrote, we also benefit from the feminist criticism that has come before us. Nina Auerbach is among the feminist critics who have thought seriously about the benefits to women of male writing and the reading of male writing. For she has identified in the greater freedom experienced by males a possibility of greater textual freedom for their female characters. Even if the sources of male writing remain impenetrable to the authors themselves, their sense of dominion in the world allows them to offer to female characters a spaciousness of vision which is indirectly enlarging to the female reader. Such critics as Rachel M. Brownstein, in *Becoming a Heroine* (Viking, 1982), testify to the use of literature as an occasion for enlarging vision and ambition for the female reader.

For women readers to look to literature for images of themselves which will contribute to their ability to analyse and to change the world, Conrad's novels provide a range of important heroic possibilities. The written texts, if cleared from their surroundings of patriarchal criticism and masculine ownership, provide for modern women readers analysis which can be empowering.

The presence of significant women characters in the works of Joseph Conrad is undeniable, though it has received little critical attention. In addition, it is regularly through those women characters that Conrad chose to express some of his most penetrating scepticism and criticism about the social and political order of Western Europe, including his adopted country of Great Britain. Creating characters who express resistance to the condition of objectification at the hands of imperialism, Conrad from the beginning of his career thus invested his women characters with critical force.[7]

Conrad was from the outset of his writing career pre-occupied with an issue which is as much central to patriarchy as it is to the strictly political world of colonialism about which Conrad wrote. That issue concerns the imposition of culture, specifically Western culture, upon the existing world of nature, specifically the natural world of the Far East or, eventually, the world of the South American silver mine. Feminist anthropology, along with feminist literary analysis, has given us awareness of some fundamental issues which point to the origins of the ideological split between nature and culture. Sherry Ortner confronts us in her ground-breaking article with the question: is nature to culture as woman is to man?[8] Is there, in other words, a long-standing association between woman and nature, each to be mastered, in its turn, by man and his artefact, culture? Is the imperialism which Conrad experienced and which he recreates in his early writing, to be understood as patriarchy (culture) struggling to master and to impose its form upon the natural, female world?

Certainly, from this perspective, the struggles between native women and white men take on a new and convincing force; the associations between native women and the jungle, the flowers, the powerful vegetation of the East, suggest from this perspective an awareness on Conrad's part of the way in which civilisation itself suffers from its mindlessly patriarchal form. As Carolyn Merchant points out early in her study of the growth of the scientific revolution, *The Death of Nature*, 'Environmentalists . . . are developing an ecological ethic emphasizing the interconnectedness between people and nature', where 'women and nature have an age-old association – an affiliation that has persisted throughout culture, language, and history.'[9] The sense of the natural world as female, a sense which underlies much of Conrad's work, was central to human thought for innumerable generations. 'The female earth was central to the organic cosmology that was undermined by the Scientific Revolution and the rise of a market-oriented culture in early modern Europe.'[10] This analysis establishes immediately the connection between a political awareness of the cost of Western culture and the ecological cost, the cost to female power and its integration into a pre-industrial way of life.

Merchant's description of European cultures prior to the scientific revolution might be accounts of the cultures which appear in Conrad's novels of colonialism in the late nineteenth century: 'technologies were low level, people considered themselves parts of a finite cosmos, and animism and fertility cults that treated nature as sacred were numerous.'[11] In his first novels, whose action takes place in the Far East that Conrad himself explored in his career as a seaman, the sexual identity of 'nature' is at issue from the outset. The native tribes themselves attribute certain natural powers and affinities to native women, while the natives in relation to the European whites are perceived by the colonisers as feminine, guileful, intuitive, and at home in an environment that resists the artefacts of 'civilisation'. The effects of rotting, drying, and disintegrating nature upon the trappings of white civilisation testify to the fearful contest between patriarchy, with its direct attack on the natural world, and native culture, which adapts and defers to the natural environment and to female power. In a recent study of the literary use of the concept of primitivism, Marianna Torgovnick suggests that 'the circularity between the concepts "female" and "primitive" is so complete in Conrad that it is difficult to tell which set of tropes influences which. Yet clearly, the feminine is perceived in the same terms used by the West for the primitive.'[12]

Some of the most thoughtful and significant feminist writing in contemporary times has not been directly focused on literature; but our reading of literature as feminists must be deeply affected by such writing. In particular, feminist discussion of the relation between women and nature, nature and patriarchal thought, and women and science have much bearing on a feminist reading of such literature as that of Joseph Conrad. For Conrad was himself deeply aware of and deeply sceptical of the focus on science and the conquest of the earth. His scepticism was both philosophical and political, similar in many ways to the feminist lines of analysis which culminate in the work of anthropologists such as Ortner and historians of science such as June Goodfield, Evelyn Fox Keller, and Carolyn Merchant. All these concentrate on deconstructing the long association between patriachy and science, between patriarchy and a natural order which assumes dominion over nature which is the female. Despite Torgovnick's scepticism, Conrad did not simply apply Western conventions about the primitive to his analysis of the Malay peninsula or Africa. Rather, he used those conventions to expose the thought patterns character-istic of Western colonialism and patriarchy, their point of departure.

Writing as he did from a position on the margin of Western thought and society, his sensibility and his nature having formed in a household and in a culture remarkably different from the conventional Western household and culture, Conrad took a stance as a writer which challenged and subverted the Western assumptions about men and nature. Imperialism, colonialism, the traffic in ivory and in silver represent in concrete political and economic terms the death of nature illuminated in Merchant's analysis of the scientific revolution.

One of the earliest principles of the new feminist move-ment was the necessity for analysis to be multi-faceted; the old discipline-based method of analysis itself was a product of hierarchical and patriarchal thought. Modes of discourse have much to say to one another. Literature, the very defini-tion of literature, had been necessarily outlined through a patriarchal order which claimed language, gender, genre, origin as its own. To demystify literature the feminist critic needed to get behind it, to unpack notions of form, character, style. Such a methodological approach has demanded, for a feminist reading of Joseph Conrad, assimilation of several modes of thought. Detached from the army of professional critics who read him through the eyes of patriarchy, including classical Freudian analysis, Conrad emerges for the feminist reader of today as a writer subversive of his adopted culture. Regularly suspicious of timely political approaches to deep-seated human problems, Conrad explored in his work the reigning assumptions about men and women, nature and culture. Close reading of his texts reveals Conrad to have been a writer who used the conventions, the subjects, and the forms of his own time as his means of reflecting back on that era and its history. From his earliest novels, which look at imperialism as the culmination of Western culture, Conrad wrote through the critical eyes of women characters, a practice he never abandoned throughout his long career.

The feminist reader of today, the beneficiary of thoughtful and complex theoretical approaches to the nature of literature itself, comes to Conrad with a profoundly new approach. It is now possible for us to reclaim that in Conrad's work which is of continuing value to feminist readers, as well as to understand the ways in which the deep strain of criticism Conrad brought to his own patriarchal world speaks to our continuing efforts to deconstruct and rebuild that world. Through narrative strategies, female characterisations, and reference to his own marginal status, Conrad found means to express in works prized by patriarchal culture a consistent and profound criticism of that very culture.

CHAPTER ONE

Conrad's Early Novels and Tales: *Almayer's Folly, An Outcast of the Islands* and *Tales of Unrest*

Of course, women characters occupy critical space in Conrad's early works. It is beyond dispute that women such as Kaspar Almayer's wife and Aissa, his lover, as well as Nina Almayer, serve to embody values, ideas and emotions central to his work. But such characters have been regularly dismissed, by the very critics who notice their presence in the novels, as poorly delineated, stereotypical, hysterical, and lifeless.[1] Analysis of these early books from a feminist and critical perspective enables us to understand and to show what lies beneath the women's characterisations which reveals such language as 'stereotypical' and 'lifeless' to be driven by critical perspectives that bring no life to readings of Conrad.

Conrad's early novels and tales examine the practice of colonialism, the tensions and subterfuges which preoccupy both the white colonisers and the native populations. As readers, we may be so drawn to the analysis of colonialism that we ignore the deeper investigation which Conrad makes into the system of which colonialism is only one manifestation: patriarchy, especially patriarchal religion, which sanctions and even outlines the form of colonialism which the early novels explore and expose. In this analysis of patriarchy, the attentive reader understands the

13

significance of the women characters in a new light, for it is they who grope to envision and articulate another sort of reality which would transcend or at least deny the struggle between white and native which absorbs energies needed (and lost) for resistance to the patriarchal system firmly in place in white cultures and to some degree binding in the native world as well.

Susan Lundvall Brodie attempts to reconcile and update earlier critical attitudes towards women in Conrad's fiction by stressing the interrelations between masculine and feminine impulses; Brodie distinguishes between 'romantic idealism', which is feminine, and 'enlightened realism, or skepticism', which is masculine. Both, she goes on to say, constitute variations on human idealism, though 'masculine ideals tend to reveal an undercurrent of egoism, a self-involvement and self-centredness notably absent in the feminine counterpart.'2 This sort of analysis tempts the reader once again to approach these texts by way of male and female roles and systems rather than through identification and analysis of the underlying structure which the roles play out. It is through the language and imagery associated with the creation and use of the river settlement of Sambir, at the hands of Captain Lingard, that Conrad reveals the coercive nature of the patriarchal world view which dominates the early novels.

Captain Tom Lingard is the father figure whose presence or absence dominates the individual and communal lives of Sambir. The texts, both around and through his voice, describe him as a patriarchal god responsible for, but not to, the world he thinks he has created. Benita Parry, a contemporary critic concerned with *Conrad and Imperialism*, discerns in Conrad a writer 'hostile' to imperialism; she notes as well his attempt to 'chronicle the lives of the colonisers as Promethean figures.' Thus, she says, 'he is obliged to show them to be fallible adventurers or impersonators of imperialism's aggressive and engorging will.'3 These characteristics of the coloniser are, once again, derived from a world view based on unselfconscious patriarchy.

Conrad notes in his Author's Note to *Almayer's Folly* that a woman, or as he says 'a lady – distinguished in the world of letters – summed up her disapproval of it by saying that the tales . . . produced were "decivilized" ' (p. vii). With some irritation, Conrad went on to remark that 'A judgment like that has nothing to do with justice.' In fact, that precise choice of language, 'decivilised', has everything to do with justice in the evaluation of these books, for the texts, read from a particular perspective, reveal themselves to illuminate a level of human behaviour that is other than 'civilised', for all the effort both whites and Malays make to claim civilisation for themselves. It is this fundamental level of treatment that the distinguished woman reader grasped and skewered with the term 'decivilised'.

Almayer's Folly and *An Outcast of the Islands* have much in common and may be discussed jointly in relation to much criticism of Conrad, including the question of 'decivilisation'. Both novels ostensibly have as their protagonists white men, protégés of Captain Lingard, who marry half-caste women, encounter the native world of the East, and are destroyed by their relations with women. But the real texts of the novels have to do with the father, his quarrelling sons, and the natural women who offer a new and different life outside the walled garden. The justly famous formulation by the anthropologist which asks whether female is to male as nature is to culture describes the scheme which structures these early novels. The men, who represent Western patriarchal culture, associate themselves with what they perceive to be civilisation. The women, half-castes or natives, are taken to be representatives of the world of nature, with all its associations of the unpredictable and the (therefore) uncontrollable. However, this set of motifs is by no means limited to a social or political level of analysis. Because Lingard is surrounded by imagery and language that intimates his status as a god, more than the 'Promethean figure' discussed by Benita Parry, it is useful to begin the analysis of Conrad's treatment of patriarchal values with some attention to Lingard.

> Knowing nothing of Arcadia – he dreamed of Arcadian happiness for that little corner of the world which he loved to think all his own. (*An Outcast of the Islands*, p. 200)

> His deep-seated and immovable conviction that only he – . . . –

he, Lingard – knew what was good for them was characteristic of him and, after all, not so very far wrong. He would make them happy whether or no, he said, and he meant it. His trade brought prosperity to the young state, and the fear of his heavy hand secured its internal peace for many years. He looked proudly upon his work. With every passing year he loved more the land, the people, the muddy river that, if he could help it, would carry no other craft but the *Flash* on its unclean and friendly surface. . . . He loved it all. . . . He loved everything there, animated or inaminated; the very mud of the riverside; the very alligators, enormous and stolid, basking on it with impertinent unconcern. . . . His thunderous laughter filled the verandah, rolled over the hotel garden, overflowed into the street, paralyzing for a short moment the noiseless traffic of brown bare feet; and its loud reverberations would even startle the landlord's tame bird – a shameless mynah – into a momentary propriety of behaviour under the nearest chair. In the big billiard-room perspiring men in thin cotton singlets would stop the game, listen, cue in hand, for a while through the open windows, then nod their moist faces at each other sagaciously and whisper: 'The old fellow is talking about his river'. (*An Outcast of the Islands*, pp. 201–2)

Lingard as a fatherly creative principle is sharply drawn in the central sections of *An Outcast of the Islands*; his unconsciousness of his own nature, or that of others, may only be described as sublime. His 'sons', Almayer and Willems, attempt from time to time to clarify for themselves and for him the nature and the effect of the dependency his lordly behaviour creates in those he commands. 'Yes! Cat, dog, anything that can scratch or bite; as long as it is harmful enough and mangy enough. A sick tiger would make you happy – of all things. . . . You haven't any pity to spare for the victims of your infernal charity. . . . Yes! It has always been so. Always. As far back as I can remember. . . . You have no morality' (*An Outcast of the Islands*, p. 162). There is desperation in Almayer's attempt to illustrate to Lingard the corrosive effects of his 'charity', which comes as a thoughtless consequence of Lingard's conception of himself as benevolent. Additionally, Lingard acts out of a half-articulated sense of his freedom from the bonds of mortality:

'If you had been in trouble as often as I have, my boy, you

wouldn't carry on so. I have been ruined more than once. Well, here I am.' (*An Outcast of the Islands*, p. 163)

This theme of the patriarchal white man's attempt to escape from the natural order is one which will be explored more particularly through the conflicts between Almayer and his daughter, Nina, and those between Willems and Aissa. But thematically Conrad regularly suggests that the male association with history and with the transcendence of time does battle with the female association with a natural order. Such opposition has its own history which extends back beyond biblical imagery to the ancient sagas of Gilgamesh and Inanna. Particular images and characterisations which take for granted this underlying set of Western assumptions will emerge most clearly in readings of passages about Almayer and Nina, Willems and Aissa.

But other recent Conrad criticism, unconcerned with issues of women, patriarchy, and feminism, has also claimed myth and religion as underpinnings for these early novels. Such a critic is Stephen K. Land, whose work was based on an analysis of *Almayer's Folly* and *An Outcast of the Islands* which locates their origins in Wagner's treatment of the *Ring* cycle.[4] While the parallels are strained, Land's insight suggests that political and personal imagery in the early novels is itself based on an already-existing set of ideas so taken for granted that Conrad uses them confidently without discussion or reference. Those ideas, about man and culture, woman and nature, are at the heart of Western religious and civil culture which Tom Lingard and his 'sons' inherit and attempt to carry with them into the alien 'natural' world of the garden of Southeast Asia. Western religious dependence upon the garden myth is complete enough so that the reader comprehends the effect of the imagery without necessary analysis. Conrad's scepticism, even so early in his career as the first two novels, informs his treatment of this mythology, as is evident in the transparent lack of insight that Captain Tom Lingard regularly displays. A god-like or Promethean creative principle of such self-congratulatory ingenuousness is in itself a powerful critique of Western patriarchal religious mythology.

Examples of Lingard's bluff incomprehension occur regularly in the early novels. In a general sense, Lingard consistently fails to understand women: he brings to the idea of women a set of stereotypical assumptions which often injure and always deny the individual woman's identity. Early in *Almayer's Folly*, Conrad provides the first account of Lingard's paternalistic and destructive intervention in the life of a young Malay woman who will become, in time, Almayer's wife. Conrad's tone, in this early passage, is as ironic as any tone to be found in a later work such as *The Secret Agent*, famous for its 'savage irony'. Chapter 2 of *Almayer's Folly* begins:

> When, in compliance with Lingard's abrupt demand, Almayer consented to wed the Malay girl, no one knew that on the day when the interesting young convert had lost all her natural relations and found a white father, she had been fighting desperately like the rest of them on board the prau, and was only prevented from leaping overboard, like the other few survivors, by a severe wound in the leg. (p. 21)

Christianity is the religion which the 'interesting young convert' is given; the loss of 'natural relations' clearly carries within the phrase more than the death of individual Malays. The Malay girl inevitably confuses the Christian God with the Rajah Laut, Tom Lingard, who first orphaned her and then immured her in the silence of the convent.

> She bore it all – the restraint and the teaching and the new faith – with calm submission, concealing her hate and contempt for all that new life. ... She called Lingard father, gently and caressingly, at each of his short and noisy visits, under the clear impression that he was a great and dangerous power it was good to propitiate. (p. 22)

The reader must wonder, to whom was the impression 'clear' that Lingard was a great power? Conrad's chosen voice suggests even in this first novel a regular discrepancy between the perception of most characters, particularly the male protagonists, and the discerning reader. Lingard's self-satisfaction, the confidence in his own providence, contrasts

sharply with the inwardness and self-concealment practised
by the Malay women, of whom the young orphan is only the
first example. 'The old seaman himself was perfectly happy',
the author observes. ' "You know I made her an orphan", he
often concluded solemnly when talking about his own
affairs.' (*Almayer's Folly*, p. 23). There is again in that
assertion the distinct implication of 'making' as a form of
creation; indeed, Lingard perceives himself as a creator, a
giver and taker away of life.

The imagery of Eden pervades the scenes of *Almayer's
Folly* in which Almayer and his docile wife, her Malay
identity demurely concealed, set up housekeeping in their
bower. The limits placed upon Almayer correspond nicely
with the limits set out in *Genesis*: knowledge of a certain
kind is outside the province of the newly-created couple.
Imperialism, like the religion of *Genesis*, demands that
critical 'knowledge' be withheld from the man and woman
as the sign of their obedience to and dependence on the
creator. In Lingard's world, it is knowledge of the secure
entrance to the river which Lingard keeps to himself; he
guards, as well, information about a source of gold, and it is
with the promise of eventual immense wealth that he gains
the filial devotion of his chosen son, Almayer.

Apart from the nuns who quietly enforce the terms of a
docile Christianity upon their initially ferocious convert,
there are no European women to exemplify or to question
the terms of Lingard's paternalistic and god-like stature.
And it is through his characterisation of several powerful
and enigmatic women that Conrad reveals both the cruelty
and, in the end, the fatuous inapplicability of the patriarchal
myth to the women of the Malay peninsula.

Although Conrad has often been criticised for the flatness
of his women characters, those in the early novels serve
notice from the first that they will argue passionately
against the falsification of such views as Lingard's (and
thus, indirectly, against the flattening views of European
imperialism). It may be that critics over the years have been
as resistant to the authenticity of the women characters or
to the provocation they offer to masculine formulations of
female character as Tom Lingard himself. For it is not only

through the rationalisation of Jocelyn Baines, claiming that *all* Conradian characters are in essence designed to embody ideas rather than to convince realistically, that the women characters of the early novels may be defended. Mrs Almayer and Nina, in the first novel, carry the weight of the novel in a variety of ways, not least by their presence in so many scenes that the first quarter of the novel must be said to be about them.

In the early pages of *Almayer's Folly*, Almayer himself is characterised as much through his fantasies about women (his mother, his wife, his daughter) as by any other means. Nina Almayer is the first major female character who serves first to embody and then to question the mixed heritage of East and West. The first sight of Nina in the text displays both Nina and Conrad's own complex mix of attitudes towards both races:

> She was tall for a half-caste, with the correct profile of the father, modified and strengthened by the squareness of the lower part of the face inherited from her maternal ancestors – the Sulu pirates. Her firm mouth, with the lips slightly parted and disclosing a gleam of white teeth, put a vague suggestion of ferocity into the impatient expression of her features. And yet her dark and perfect eyes had all the tender softness common to Malay women, but with a gleam of superior intelligence. (pp. 16–17)

The voice of the author here struggles for mastery over the ambiguity of Nina's heritage and stature; given Almayer's weakness and self-righteousness, the 'correct profile' with which he has endowed Nina cannot signify virtue. Yet her ancestors, pirates, can hardly be put forward unambiguously as her highest sources of value without, for Conrad, a commitment towards the objects of imperialism which he is not entirely ready to make. And whose is the 'superior intelligence' which gleams from her otherwise typically soft Malay woman's face? The syntax is ambiguous here, indicating the author's ambivalence: the superior intelligence may in fact be Nina's own, part of the essence of her individuality. But it may just as well be that of her father's race, redeeming her from the mindlessness of the Malay

woman her father married at the behest of his adoptive
father. The reader, a 'resisting reader', perhaps, can find in
this description encouragement for a reading of Nina
focused on thoughtful individuality. At the same time, the
reader must be alert to the perils of the author who
struggles to distance himself from the very paradigms he
attempts to dissect. The complex and unclear position of the
author towards the Malay woman is vividly exposed to the
reader in another early passage from *Almayer's Folly*: in
this passage, Conrad describes the disintegration of the
relationship between Almayer and Nina's mother. What is
remarkable is the number of times that the word 'savage'
appears in the passages, always as an adjective. 'His wife
soon commenced to treat him with a savage contempt
expressed by sulky silence, only occasionally varied by
outbursts of savage invective' (op. cit. p. 25). Scarcely a page
later, Almayer attributes the term to his wife in his
thoughts, seeing her as the 'savage tigress' enraged by the
theft of her cub.

A novel consciously written to examine the effects of
imperialism upon both its bearers and its objects surely
betrays a provocative intent by such lavish use of such a
value-laden adjective. The author struggles both to delineate
the character and to distance himself from his creation:
'Almayer, sitting huddled on a pile of mats, thought with
dread of the separation with the only human being he loved
– with greater dread still, perhaps, of the scene with his
wife, the savage tigress deprived of her young. She will
poison me, thought the poor wretch, well aware of that easy
and final manner of solving the social, political, or family
problems in Malay life' (op. cit., pp. 26–7). The author
hovers over this passage, at once within Almayer's thoughts
and outside them; Almayer is a poor wretch to himself but
even poorer to the author's voice. 'That easy and final
manner' has so far been exhibited more as white dispatch
than as Malay callousness; the desperate grief of Nina's
mother, seeing her daughter effectively kidnapped from her
to be taken to Singapore and educated as a white woman,
hardly testifies to easy detachment. Conrad picks his way
along a treacherous path of narration; the liberal use of

'savage' in the thoughts and language of Almayer suggest to the reader his inability to understand or to identify with the passionate nature of his wife as girl, woman, mother. Almayer's poverty of imagination, supposedly his strong suit, diminishes his stature as protagonist while it invites the reader to wrestle with the meaning of 'savagery' in this context. Imperialism ceases to be an economic system of abstract implications and becomes, instead, the sharply focused abduction of the raw material of female children. Moral, ethical, and political issues are expressed and explored through the conflicts between men and women. The men, whether fatuously self-confident like Tom Lingard, or self-deluded and ethically stunted like Almayer, regularly must encounter the clear challenges of women who embody the issues of colonialism. But these women are by no means portrayed as passive victims: from the earliest scenes in *Almayer's Folly*, the women characters resist capture and easy classification. Both within native culture and in the homes and temples of European culture, the women characters devise patterns of evasion and revenge.

Conrad notes wryly of Mrs Almayer that she contemplated her 'little brass cross' with 'superstitious awe'. That cross, and the recollection of threats by the Mother Superior, 'were Mrs Almayer's only theological outfit for the stormy road of life.' Her daughter, Nina, did not even have that much tangible evidence to remind her of ten years of education in the white world of Singapore (p. 41). Mrs Almayer, formerly the fiercely scrapping Malay girl, never has a first name of her own. While there has been much critical speculation about the sources and implication of names in Conrad,[5] there has not been much discussion about the absence of a name for Almayer's wife: she is identified by her relationships (Nina's mother, for instance) and by her behaviour as observed by males, but what she cannot be, finally, is her particular self *as named*.

In her 1985 article, 'Women's texts', Gayatri Chakravorty Spivak discusses the consequences for 'third-world' women of appropriation, false representation at the hands of white male Western authors and feminist critics alike. Whether naming or depersonalising, Spivak suggests, the white

Westerner necessarily does violence to the woman herself, and readers need to become and to remain conscious of their own complicity in the process of objectifying those who are subjects in their own right.[6] Here, in his first novel, Conrad confronts immediately his difficult relation to the person of Mrs Almayer. There is an implicit confession of lack of empathy in the kind of non-naming that Conrad practises towards Mrs Almayer: like Mrs Vinck, the white middle-class woman who takes Nina's education in hand, the character resists the author's presentation. At the same time, however, the failure to name is a sort of choice which allows the author to relinquish his pretence to omniscience. This, in Conrad's hands, amounts to an honest denial: the author does not pretend to know who Mrs Almayer is to herself. As readers, noticing the lack of a name for this woman, we are able to do as Spivack suggests: 'develop a strategy rather than a theory of reading that might be a critique of imperialism.'[7]

Both Mrs Almayer and Nina serve in the text of *Almayer's Folly* to pose active alternatives to the white colonialists who attempt to rule; they are notable for their intimate connection and for a communication which acknowledges and overcomes their differences. Nina's youth was spent in the same kind of acute conflict and self-suppression as her mother's. Like her mother, she was taken from her natural environment by Captain Lingard to be acculturated as a European. Conrad's account of Nina's emotional turmoil suggests an empathy with her situation and none of his typical ironic detachment of tone or diction:

> For years she had stood between her mother and her father, the one so strong in her weakness, the other so weak where he could have been strong. Between those two beings so dissimilar, so antagonistic, she stood with mute heart wondering and angry at the fact of her own existence. . . . She had little belief and no sympathy for her father's dreams; but the savage ravings of her mother chanced to strike a responsive chord, deep down somewhere in her despairing heart; and she dreamed dreams of her own with the persistent absorption of a captive thinking of liberty within the walls of his prison cells. (*Almayer's Folly*, pp. 151–2)

It is Nina's response to the Malay, Dain Maroola, which brings her to an awareness and an appreciation of her mother's wisdom which is no longer characterised as 'savage'. What Conrad suggests in the differing responses of Nina's parents to her relationship with Dain is the greater value and influence of the Malay woman in relation to the men of her tribe. Almayer's horrified account of the future awaiting Nina with Dain is in fact a description of the fate of his own wife: the litany of what becomes of the native woman turned over to a European husband. ' "Do you know what is waiting for you if you follow that man? Have you no pity for yourself? Do you know that you shall be first his plaything and then a scorned slave, a drudge, and a servant of some new fancy of that man?" ' (*Almayer's Folly*, p. 178). It is characteristic of the white European to project onto the Malay his own lack of commitment to his wife, to describe as 'savagery' what is in fact 'civilised' treatment of one's wife. Nina's mother suggests a more realistic and thoughtful future for her daughter, one which represents changes in love and relationship. As their colloquy begins, Conrad notes simply that 'the two women had met behind the house', suggesting the equality and the affinity between mother and daughter on their own soil.

Conrad's sense of the bond between mother and daughter is strong but unsentimental. Mrs Almayer carries the resentment of the early years when her daughter was taken to Singapore to be made European. ' "You were his daughter then; you are my daughter now" ' (op. cit., p. 150). Knowing in her flesh the cost of imperialism, the mother entreats her daughter to give up her old life. ' "Forget you ever looked at a white face" ', she urges. ' "Forget their words; forget their thoughts. They speak lies. And they think lies because they despise us that are better than they are but not so strong. Forget their friendship and their contempt; forget their many gods" ' (op. cit., p. 151). In this crucial conversation, as the mother sends her daughter off to her Malay lover, the moral and political dimension of the women's lives emerges clearly.

One of the important challenges to the dominance of white European colonialism is the analysis of the Malay or half-caste woman; in *Almayer's Folly*, Nina Almayer and her mother achieve their closeness and their separate maturity through their resistance to white men. Aissa, in *An Outcast of the Islands*, will carry that analysis forward. But it is Conrad's achievement, if not his conscious intention, to have provided in his first novel women characters who embody the criticism and the alternatives to white, male, European self-centredness. Egoism, as analysed by critics such as Susan Brodie, is not in Conrad's work equally characteristic of male and female; more importantly, self-analysis and introspection are not equally apportioned. The typical male protagonist, in a Conrad novel, most especially those of the earliest years, may possess what Conrad terms 'imagination', but not self-awareness. The sublime self-confidence of Tom Lingard comfortably masks and projects an equally sublime lack of self-consciousness. Such absence of complexity cannot provide the 'realistic enlightenment' that Brodie and other critics claim for the masculine protagonists. Self-deluded and infatuated as they are, such men cannnot imagine the complexity of others, such as the calculating and thoughtful women who observe and analyse men's behaviour from behind curtains, veils, and shutters Nina's true heritage from her mother is her calculation, her self-knowledge, and her ability to assess her situation and her lover with detachment and rueful accuracy. While Conrad notes Dain's rapture at the feet of Nina, he notes as well Nina's sense of sadness:

> As she glanced down at his kneeling form she felt a great pitying tenderness for that man she was used to call – even in her thoughts – the master of her life. She lifted her eyes and looked sadly at the southern heavens under which lay the path of their lives – her own and that man's at her feet. (*Almayer's Folly*, p. 172)

The sadness and pity refer to the acute discrepancy between the heroic ideal of mastery and the actual dependency of the man at her feet. The women characters, whether white, half-caste, or Malay, have in common that rueful understanding of their disguised strength through which they manipulate and even control the men who dream of glory

and power. Nina, like other women characters in these early
novels, has a comprehensive understanding of her lover;
while the women are, to the men, alien and even intimidating
creatures, the men are no enigmas to the women. Nina
reflects, as she walks into the darkness of the jungle with
Dain, that 'He was hers with all his qualities and his faults.
His strength and his daring, his simple wisdom and his
savage cunning – all were hers' (op. cit., p. 172). Half white,
she has a subtle appreciation of another meaning for that
key term, 'savage'. But Dain has no such apprehension of
Nina, who is to him simply a goddess. For male characters,
Conrad suggests, women are not so much human companions
as they are embodiments of male fantasy and terror. Since
the women reveal themselves to the attentive reader as
complex, thoughtful, sceptical humans, the difference between their portrayal by the author and their perception by
the European males offers new evidence of Conrad's intentions for these characters. That difference between their
inner lives and their lives at the hands of men serves to
underline the blindness of the male characters. Even in
their awareness of their senses, the women show greater
subtlety and intelligence. At the end of her reunion with
Dain, it is Nina who hears the faint sounds from the river
that announce their pursuit. Women's sensitivity is not
restricted to the emotional sphere, nor is it limited to the
natural world as opposed to the social or political. In these
early novels, women are quite simply more self-aware and
more generally perceptive than men, and their perceptive-
ness eventually expands to become the explicit condemnation of the system of exploitation which captures the loyalty
and the imagination of the men of Europe.

Nina Almayer chooses to leave the white world with her
Malay lover, but not before offering an alternative to her
father: what she offers is self-determination and freedom
from dependence upon Lingard and European values. For a
brief and wrenching moment, Almayer contemplates the
possibility of accepting Nina and Dain into his life, and the
novel hesitates, risking its momentum in a paragraph of
agonised vacillation:

'I cannot', he muttered to himself. After a long pause he spoke again, a little lower, but in an unsteady voice. 'It would be too great a disgrace. I am a white man.' He broke down completely there, and went on tearfully, 'I am a white man, and of good family. Very good family', he repeated, weeping bitterly. 'It would be a disgrace . . . all over the island, . . . the only white man on the east coast. No, it cannot be . . . white men finding my daughter with this Malay. My daughter!' (*Almayer's Folly*, p. 184)

This unsteady prose captures the fragmented and incomplete nature of Almayer's thought as he struggles to efface Nina's identity and, a moment later, her very existence. In a reduction of male practice, this agonised father determines not only to erase Nina's reality by forgetting her name, but he works to deny her past relation to himself as well. 'He never had a daughter. He would forget. He was forgetting already' (op. cit., p. 196). What Conrad demonstrates here is the necessity for the deluded man to wipe the earth clean of the woman who pierces the delusion; and, in these books, it is always women who break through such determined unreality. The departure from the white man's garden involves risk and danger; Nina is the first Conradian heroine to break free and to offer freedom to her white father. For Almayer such freedom means death: 'His face was like the face of a man that has died struck from behind – a face from which all feelings and all expression are suddenly wiped off by the hand of unexpected death' (op. cit., p. 196).

With the development of his second novel, *An Outcast of the Islands*, Conrad created a more overt critique of white imperialism as a male experience derived from a set of age-old beliefs and practices about both women and the natural world. As Conrad describes himself in the Author's Note to this novel, there is a strong hint of the masculine creation principle at work: 'The discovery of new values in life is a very chaotic experience; there is a tremendous amount of jostling and confusion and a momentary feeling of darkness. I let my spirit float supine over that chaos' (op. cit., p. vii).

From the outset, *An Outcast of the Islands* makes visible the deep contradictions implicit in the anti-imperialist stance which Conrad adopted even as he began, in his personal life, the attempt to find a niche in British intellectual and economic life. That ambivalence may be illustrated by Conrad's remark that 'the story itself was never very near my heart. It engaged my imagination much more than my affections' (op. cit., p. ix). The original of Willems, the outcast of the title, was characterised by Conrad as interesting by virtue of his 'dependent position, his strange, dubious, status of a mistrusted, disliked, worn-out European', language remarkably suggestive of Conrad's own anomalous status in England in 1919 when he wrote the introductory remarks from a calculated distance.

Conrad gave to Willems the recognisable signs of late-Victorian self-righteousness and mysogynistic self-indulgence. No intellectual, Willems muses on a debased version of the self-satisfied Spenserian version of Darwinism: 'The wise, the strong, the respected, have no scruples. Where there are scruples there can be no power. On that text he preached often to the young men. It was his doctrine, and he, himself, was a shining example of its truth' (*An Outcast of the Islands*, p. 8). The banality of the language attributed to Willems displays his shallow intellect and the depth of his ignorance. It is not surprising that he abuses his wife both physical'y and emotionally, nor that he is known to do so without incurring any penalty. ' "Horrid man", said Mrs Vinck calmly. "I have heard he beats his wife." "Oh no, my dear", muttered absently Mr Vinck, with a vague gesture. "The aspect of Willems as a wife-beater presented to him no interest' (op. cit., p. 10). In an age and a culture in which violence within the home was virtually endemic, Willems' participation in the practice evokes no special reaction. Vinck's further thought, 'How women do misjudge', allows Conrad to comment editorially on the Vincks' relationship as well. 'If Willems wanted to torture his wife he would have recourse to less primitive methods.' Early on, then, the novel establishes western civilisation and the supposedly primitive as both synonymous and opposed. The barbarity at the heart of European civilisation, which critics anatomise in *Heart of Darkness*, is in fact laid bare in the early pages of *An Outcast of the Islands*. Since domestic violence was so characteristic of British households, and since Willems and Vinck desired nothing more than to represent the British norm, this early exchange lays the groundwork for the exposure not merely of the flaws in Willems' character, as critics would have it, but rather for the barbarism at the heart of the imperial model. It is this kind of penetration that a feminist analysis can provide, seizing upon the violence within marriage as the key to the desires as well as the characters that exemplify imperialism.

In the second novel, women take on greater importance in the analysis of imperialism; at the same time, the depiction of the individual woman taxes Conrad's abilities as a writer. In this novel, women speak to the reader in a number of different modes: in their own voices, through the narrator's voice, and through the understanding of the male characters. What we as readers understand is often at sharp variance from the understanding of Willems, the protagonist; as a result, we judge him flawed and sharply limited. His radical misreading of his wife, attributing to her apparent passivity a respect for him which she never entertained, places Willems perfectly in the mainstream of nineteenth-century, middle-class, British male thinking. When Willems forces himself to tell his wife the news of his (and, he thinks, their) financial catastrophe, brought on by his own dishonesty, he expects abject despair; he receives withering scorn. ' "Oh! You great man!" she said distinctly, but in a voice that was hardly above a whisper' (*An Outcast of the Islands*, p. 27).

Being used to the idea of his wife as a veritable extension of himself, Willems experiences this response in amazement. 'Those words, and still more her tone, stunned him as if somebody had fired a gun close to his ear. He stared back at her stupidly' (op. cit., p. 27). Women's individuality thus becomes an issue in the novel as a challenge to the white male's sense of himself and of the order in the world. The mode of hierarchy suggests not only an order of being but a world of being in which the wife and the child are extensions, projections, of the male husband and father. Joanna's language: 'You are nobody now', suggests starkly the problem these novels explore. Relationships of unequal power serve to enhance the identity of the men, and it is this sense of existence which is imperilled by the woman's autonomy. ' "Do not speak to me" ', Joanna continues. ' "I have heard what I waited for all these years. You are less than dirt, you that have wiped your feet on me. I have waited for this. I am not afraid now" ' (op. cit., p. 27). Conrad suggests that Willems' sense of his own identity is so fragile that he literally disappears to himself when confronted by the rebellion of a newly strong woman. The encounter with his wife prefigures the later descent into terror when Aissa offers herself to him without reservation. In each case, Willems loses confidence in his own existence in the face of an empowered woman.

In the character of Aissa, Conrad created a woman of enormous charm and beauty who attracts and terrifies both Willems, her lover, and the author. In an early passage, Conrad writes that to Aissa Willems was a man 'with all the fascination of a great and dangerous thing . . . [with] all the attractiveness of the vague and the unknown – of the unforeseen and the sudden; of a being strong, dangerous, alive, and human, ready to be enslaved' (An Outcast of the Islands, p. 75). That desire to enslave is not innate to Aissa but is attributed to her by men, from Willems to the native go-between, Babalatchi, to the author. Aissa's effect upon Willems from the first is captivating: 'in the sudden darkness of her going he would be left weak and helpless, as though despoiled violently of all that was himself' (op. cit., p. 77). Briefly, Willems determines to extricate himself from Aissa's intoxication:

> He had a sudden moment of lucidity – of that cruel lucidity that comes once in a life to the most benighted. He seemed to see what went on within him, and was horrifed at the strange sight. He, a white man whose worst fault till then had been a little want of judgment and too much confidence in the rectitude of his kind! That woman was a complete savage, and . . . (An Outcast of the Islands, p. 80)

Here the issue of clarity is as critical as that of savagery. Conrad has already indicated that Willems exists in a haze of self-delusion, that he is a bully, and that he fears loss of face more than the violation of ethical distinctions. Within this passage, then, is the character's shock of recognition, itself wholly flawed. The opposition of civilisation and savagery, so important to this book, is always subject to the irony of attribution.

Conrad, having become by now thoroughly familiar with the British tradition of literary imperialism, struggles to articulate his own critical understanding. That struggle is inextricably bound up with his treatment of the character of Aissa. Benita Parry, in her study of Conrad and imperialism, agrees with earlier critics that Conrad's attitudes were influenced by his friend, Cunninghame Graham. At the same time, however, Parry contends that Conrad attributed 'immutable properties to the colonial worlds, where the unreconstructed landscapes transfigure the planet's prehistory and symbolize moral vacancy, the archaic social arrangements are the extant form of the primal condition and the peoples personify a state of stupefied unconsciousness.'[8] Following the line of Bernard Meyer's earlier 'Psychoanalytic biography', Parry and other critics view Aissa as an example of Conrad's own hysteria about devouring women. In addition, Parry criticises Conrad's stance as inadvertent 'illuminations of the imperialist imagination rather than . . . critical reflections of the corporate consciousness of imperialism, for the demystification of the colonialist benevolence is eclipsed by the mystification of the East as a force of primal evil. . . . Such is the context in which the encounter between East and West unfolds, where the "corrupt" love that flares up between Malayan women and white men is further vitiated by mutual incomprehension . . . and is doomed to end in a hatred born of race and blood.'[9]

Such criticism, more recently proposed by Marianna Torgovnick in her study of *Heart of Darkness* in *Gone Primitive: Savage Intellects, Modern Lives* suggests both that Conrad was helpless against his own compulsions and that he wrote as a generalist; neither of these descriptions adequately accounts for the powerful presence of Aissa and the particular relationship she and Willems undertake. In the novels there is in fact only one 'corrupt' love, and it serves to illuminate the long-standing assumptions about natural women and civilising men which Conrad questions in the unfolding of the novel. The descriptions of Aissa and the febrile jungle are those of Willems, hardly the *alter ego* of the author. 'Willems measured dismally the depth of his degradation. He – a white man, the admired of white men, was held by these miserable savages whose tool he was about to become. He felt for them all the hate of his race, of his morality, of his intelligence. He looked upon himself with dismay and pity' (*An Outcast of the Islands*, p. 127). This particularity of observation serves to undermine every judgement in the passage, so that the words recoil upon the character. Judgements about Conrad's own complicity with imperialism and with portrayals of devouring women must be made in conjunction with both close reading and a sense of Conrad's own history as a person deeply familiar with the consequences of such stereotypical thinking. Neither Parry nor Torgovnick consider the effects of characterisation on pronouncements about the feverish and corrupting nature of the jungle.

In the end, the behaviour and speech of Aissa, themselves, determine the effect of her character within the text and upon the reader. Although critics ordinarily describe Aissa in terms of her relationship with Willems, it is the challenge and confrontation she offers to Lingard which carries out the critique of patriarchal Western values. Aissa quite literally does not speak the language in which Lingard and Willems play out their drama of prodigal son and self-righteous father. The masculine and closed universe in which Lingard commands and controls suffers irreversible damage at the angry entry of Aissa: seeking access to Lingard's mind, Aissa 'exploded into pained fury so violent that it drove Lingard back a pace, like an unexpected blast of wind. He lifted both hands, incongruously paternal in his venerable aspect, bewildered and soothing, while she stretched her neck forward and shouted at him' (op. cit., p. 251).

This scene of furious dialogue forces on the reader, as on Tom Lingard, the unveiled passion of Aissa; her self-disclosure, more than Willems has been able to receive, spills into halting and penetrating language.

'Go away.... Forget him.... He has no courage and no wisdom any more ... and I have lost my power.... Go away and forget. There are other enemies. Leave him to me. He had been a man once.... You are too great. Nobody can withstand you'. (*An Outcast of the Islands*, p. 253)

Interestingly, Lingard reflects that, 'Unexpectedly he had come upon a human being – a woman at that – who had made him disclose his will before its time' (op. cit., p. 255). This bewilderment is Lingard's, not the author's. What Aissa has flung at Lingard is her self, piercing even his armour of incomprehension. When he attempts to control her passionate and demonstrative behaviour – ' "Get out of my path. You ... ought to know that when men meet in daylight women must be silent and abide their fate" ' – Aissa responds with a tirade of focused fury. ' "Yes, I am a woman" ', she begins, but her outburst rapidly ascends to a new level of challenge. In a burst of articulate detail, Aissa describes her participation in the battles of her culture against white men, while men died beside her. ' "And from their cold hands [I] took the paddle and worked so that those with me did not know that one more man was dead. I did all this. What more have you done? That was my life. What has been yours?" ' (op. cit., p. 246).

With such rich illustration of Aissa's mental and emotional power of analysis and speech, what explains the generations of critical disparagement and scorn for the character and for Conrad's achievement? A recent critic, Helen Funk Rieselbach, echoes earlier assessments of Conrad when she notes that relations between parents and children are 'problematic' and 'love relationships between adult men and women are fraught with danger. Women are seen as threatening presences or as predestined victims.' Predictably, she goes on to cite Bernard C. Meyer's observation that 'traditional sex roles are often reversed', so that the heroines become 'potentially threatening.'[10]

Surely, along with Willems, it is the Conradian critics
who have been threatened by the characterisation of Aissa.
It is certainly overstatement, and demonstrably inaccurate,
to describe the women of these first two novels as *either*
threatening forces *or* predestined victims. Both Almayer
and Willems, along with Lingard, experience radical dis-
orientation precisely because women – their wives, daughters
and lovers – fail to conform to such either/or stereotyping.
Critics who attribute such polarities of thought to Conrad
seem to bring those assumptions to the texts. 'Conrad
depicts Willems' love for Aissa as a turning towards moral
decay and darkness. . . . Like Sambir her façade is appealing,
while containing the threat of the forbidden and destructive.'[11] Like Meyer's early attempt to criticise Conrad's
work through a crude Freudian assessment, Daniel Schwartz
brings to the discussion of these early novels assumptions
which equate sexuality with self-condemnation for Conrad.
'The man who violates sacrosanct moral laws', writes
Schwarz, 'brings upon himself his own nemesis.'[12] Nemesis,
in this instance, is presumably the liaison with a 'devouring'
Aissa, while 'sacrosanct moral laws' describe the marriage
sacrament which allows Willems to terrorise his wife until
she seizes her moment of self-assertion. Frederick R. Karl,
in *Joseph Conrad: The Three Lives*, views the relationship
between Aissa and Willems as that of a 'man haunted by a
woman and eventually destroyed by her extraordinary
needs, which he cannot fulfill.'[13] Karl attributes this
characterisation to Conrad's recent marriage and the result-
ing fears and anxieties of woman as the 'other', anxieties so
fierce that they produced successive portraits of ferocious
women who served more as projections of Conrad's anxieties
than as characters in their own right. Such a reading
depends on a biographical approach which is both incorrect
and critically limiting.

In short, it seems that there has been and continues to be
a sharp disparity between the contents of these first two
novels and the critical perception of them. The novels
subvert, question, and largely invalidate the imperialist
and patriarchal assumptions of Conrad's adopted culture
of England and Western Europe. They illuminate the

bonds between mothers and daughters, among natives, and between women and their culturally derived strengths. Savagery, attributed by the colonialists to the female figures, regularly recoils upon the observers to describe more accurately their despoilation of the land and the inhabitants of the East. Critics seem to project onto the texts the very Western patriarchal values from which the protagonists suffer and which Conrad shows to be destructive to women and men alike.

The powerful and misrepresented women in the early novels of Conrad deserve our attention, in the face both of critics hostile to the subversive nature of the texts and the devotion of feminist energies to male writers. Thus, Nina and Aissa must struggle for proper understanding also at the hands of influential and important feminist critics such as Elaine Showalter who writes with alarm at the 'post-feminist spirit' which 'translates into pressure to stop working on women and to work once more on the real literature, the important writers, which is to say the traditional male canon.'[14] Women, here, must come to mean those women such as Aissa, Nina, the nameless Mrs Almayer, who call to us for understanding. Those women deserve to find readers of Conrad who respond to his effort to give voice to all those who resisted the powerful lure of the very culture which enticed him as well: patriarchal Western imperialism, the domain of Tom Lingard and his sons.

CHAPTER TWO

Men Without Women

The novels and tales which are usually taken to be Conrad's major early works, from 'Youth' to *Lord Jim*, appear to be those least hospitable to women and to feminist analysis. Indeed, most readers take this group of tales to be entirely representative of Conrad's career, ignoring the works that preceded them and many of those that followed. This focus accounts for the simplistic and incorrect perception of Conrad as a writer of sea stories, but it also distorts his position as a thoughtful questioner and analyst of British hierarchical culture, precisely the kind of analysis that recent feminist literary criticism has developed in regard to other major writers. It is important here to demonstrate that it is not simply the presence of women as characters within a text which makes the text susceptible to feminist analysis; rather, we can observe within texts such as *Heart of Darkness* and *Lord Jim* illumination of the roles that women played in the imagination both of the author and of the culture out of which he wrote, even when the women as characters exist only briefly and fitfully in what Conrad might call a 'veiled visage'. Indeed, in these great tales of the river and the sea, certain redemptive qualities may be regularly identified, most especially an unsentimental but tender clarity of understanding, which enables the reader to achieve both the empathy and the distance necessary for full understanding of the dilemmas posed both by civilisation and the natural world.

Both nature and the ship have traditionally been identified

with the female principle in Western culture and literature; these works by Conrad rely heavily on those long-attributed meanings. There is an equally traditional opposition posed between the intuitive, irrational East and the ordered rationality of the West; Conrad's 'veiled bride' repeatedly serves that set of polarities. However, it has been the critical interpretation of these key texts, more than the texts themselves, which has contributed to the image of Conrad as a writer both incapable of creating complex female characters and uninterested in such characters because they are not part of the sea-going world. In fact, these novels contain many suggestions of female alternatives to the male orthodoxy, natural as well as political, developing from Conrad's earlier narrative techniques and his growing sense of commitment to his life on the land in Britain. *Heart of Darkness* offers perhaps the clearest indication of this complex set of attitudes.

In the earliest novels, women characters served to criticise the dominant mode of political and moral thought; in their words and by their lives they offered alternative visions. In the novels and tales which follow, Conrad turns to a new narrative method which, in effect, compensates for the absence of fully developed and integrated female characters: the unnamed male narrator of *The Nigger of the 'Narcissus'* and Charlie Marlow of *Heart of Darkness* and *Lord Jim*.

For many critics, this group of works by Conrad announces his attainment of narrative mastery; these are the novels and tales which testify to his artistic maturity and achievement of focus. Their evidence of that maturity and focus may be seen in the new stage of development in Conrad's effort to think himself free of the temptations and constraints of Western imperialist thought. In her analysis of this subject, the critic Benita Parry identifies Conrad's particular marginality as a condition contributing to his inclination and his ability to perform such analysis. 'Because he lived on the borderlines of various traditions', she writes, 'Conrad occupied a vantage point beyond the outlook of disaffected political writers who like him reviled the materialism of their society, deplored the motives of a ruthless colonialism and were alarmed at the flagrant chauvinism this had excited, but believed imperialism to be a malaise within capitalism.'[1] What Parry does not go on to say, and what a different analysis does seem to show, is that Conrad succeeded in *Lord Jim* and in *Heart of Darkness* in pillorying not the absence of Western humanitarian values in the male colonisers, but rather the presence of such values and their destructive effect on Western man and colonised native alike. Such a revelation is not, as Parry and others suggest, reserved for Marxist thinkers; the texts show other ways to judge imperialism and societies on land or sea organised along traditional hierarchical principles. Through women characters, or through male assessments of women's roles and natures, Conrad seems to have been able to contemplate the nature of Western culture, about which he was always deeply ambivalent. Critics who object to the portrayals of love, that 'uncongenial subject', as Thomas Moser characterised it, do not make the connection between the focus on women and the analysis of cultural values. In fact, Moser wonders:

> . . . why Conrad, rather than subordinating women and love in the full-length novels, did not cut them out altogether and produce only perfect works like *The Nigger of the 'Narcissus'* and 'The Secret Sharer.' One can only assume the subject seemed to him a necessary condition of painting on a canvas broader than that of a short novel. Such a feeling would hardly make Conrad unique among novelists. Except for *Moby Dick*, it is difficult to name a major novel that completely avoids women and love.[2]

Along with Bernard Meyer, who in 1967 published a study of Conrad ostensibly based on psychoanalytic principles, Moser and some other male critics focus on what they see as Conrad's fears and ambivalence towards women and sexuality. The 'perfection' of a work such as 'The Secret Sharer' thus depends upon its clear-cut masculinity, its unmixed focus on the male rite of passage which releases the nervous young captain into adult command of his ship through the taking on and the casting off of the male *alter ego*, Leggatt.

But the famous novels and tales of this period cannot

absolutely avoid the female, even when she is not present in the disturbing form of the articulate native woman of the earlier novels. Conrad struggles to articulate a value system in *The Nigger of the 'Narcissus'* which will express the manliness of solidarity and truth in the face of dissolution and death. To do so, he wrestles with definitions that come perilously close to polarities of sex- or gender-based extremities. Community is necessary on board the ship, and community is based in great measure on male bonding. But the same community which supports the ship's endeavours and defers to 'her' supreme needs, defers as well to Jimmy Wait's 'shameless' demoralisation, his denial of his own approaching death. These central pages of *The Nigger of the 'Narcissus'*, in which the Captain quells the mutinous mood and Jimmy lies silently before his fate, demonstrate Conrad's early attempts to sort out and attribute virtue according to a set of assumptions about gender and human values. Tenderness and compassion, properly expressed by women, here unman and undercut truth and fidelity:

> It was at that time that Belfast's devotion – and also his pugnacity – secured universal respect. He spent every moment of his spare time in Jimmy's cabin. He tended to him, talked to him; was as gentle as a woman, as tenderly gay as an old philanthropist, as sentimentally careful of his nigger as a model slave-owner. (*The Nigger of the 'Narcissus'*, p. 140)

Compensating outside the cabin for his tremendous forbearance and consideration, Belfast behaves with additional belligerence towards the rest of the crew. As many critics have realised, community and social values lie at the heart of this short novel. A more subtle question of values, however, has to do with the definitions of manhood, manliness, and health, none of which can finally be attained without the internalisation of some of the capacities ordinarily reserved for women and womanhood.

In their care for the ship, the men of the 'Narcissus' look to her for direction and preservation; hungering for food, they 'went on scraping, polishing, painting the ship from morning to night. And soon she looked as thought she had come out of a bandbox; but hunger lived on board of her' (op. cit.,

p. 143). The attentions are to the surface here, to the appearance of this vital female. Regularly they test the ship's ability to save them, but 'she seemed to have forgotten the way home . . . She ran backwards and forwards, distracted, like a timid creature at the foot of a wall' (op. cit., p. 143). In this mode, behaving with traditional chivalric regard for the feminine, the men continue hungry and distracted. Not until they have been reduced to frightened children, consigning the body of James Wait to the depths of the sea, will the ship take hold again as their maternal safety. The scene in which Wait's sail-wrapped body resists being tipped into the ocean calls forth from the men all their pretences of brave solidarity; it is their depths which are plumbed. Belfast speaks for them all when he shrieks, ' "Jimmy, be a man" ', and ' "Go, Jimmy! – Jimmy, go! Go" ' (op. cit., p. 160). At the eventual departure of Wait's corpse, 'the crowd stepped forward like one man.'

Contrary to the perfection ascribed by critics such as Moser to the writing in *The Nigger of the 'Narcissus'*, the writing style is often awkward and confused, overwrought and even inaccurate, as in the critical moment of Wait's burial at sea. 'The grey package started reluctantly to whizz off the lifted planks all at once, with the suddenness of a flash of lightning.' The awkwardness of that description, with whizzing and reluctance juxtaposed against one another, is just one example of infelicity.

It is, of course, their deaths which the men must face as individuals and as a community; they must at the same time continue to function as a crew if the ship is to help them save themselves. As the femaleness of the 'Narcissus' required recognition and deference, so eventually does the femaleness of the earth itself, not apparent until the later sections of the text. Until then, the antipathy between the sea and the land seems to govern the text, with the virtues of the sea posed against the amusements and unrest of the land. But in the ship's approach to port up through the Channel, the land itself emerges as a great female ship. 'The dark land lay alone in the midst of waters, like a mighty ship bestarred with vigilant lights – a ship freighted with dross and with jewels, with gold and with steel. She towered up

immense and strong, guarding priceless traditions and
untold suffering, sheltering glorious memories and base
forgetfulness, ignoble virtues and splendid transgressions.
A great ship!' (op. cit., pp. 162–3). Conrad may wish to
glorify or at least commemorate the valour and the tenuous
community of the men who go to sea together under sail.
But his valedictory tone at the conclusion of *The Nigger of
the 'Narcissus'* succeeds rather in emphasising the childlike
qualities of the men in their dependence upon the female
qualities of their ship and the land itself. Even the vignette
of Charley in the grip of his mother contributes to this
ambivalent portrait:

> As I came up I saw a red-faced, blowsy woman, in a grey shawl,
> and with dusty, fluffy hair, fall on Charley's neck. It was his
> mother. She slobbered over him: 'O, my boy! My boy!' – 'Leggo
> of me,' said Charley, 'Leggo, mother!' I was passing him at
> the time, and over the untidy head of the blubbering woman he
> gave me a humorous smile and a glance ironic, courageous,
> and profound, that seemed to put all my knowledge of life to
> shame. I nodded and passed on, but heard him say again, good-
> naturedly: – 'If you leggo of me this minyt – ye shall have five
> bob for a drink out of my pay.' (op. cit., p. 171)

However affectionate the portrait may have been that was
intended by the author, the men emerge in the language of
the text as incomplete, immature, and unsteady on their
feet. The nostalgia of the narrator suffuses the final page of
the text, but it cannot obscure the cumulative effect of the
novel which conveys quite a different composite portrait. In
the farewell, the narrator addresses the men of the 'Narcissus'
with fond recollection:

> Haven't we, together and upon the immortal sea, wrung out a
> meaning from our sinful lives? Good-bye, brothers! You were a
> good crowd. As good a crowd as ever fisted with wild cries the
> beating canvas of a heavy foresail; or tossing aloft, invisible in
> the night, gave back yell for yell to a westerly gale. (op. cit.,
> p. 173)

Of course, the crew of the 'Narcissus' succeeded in none of

those endeavours: faced with the life and death of James Wait, the crew fragmented and lost its precious solidarity. Individually vulnerable, the members of the crew looked for meaning and moral leadership to its most visible members: Singleton, Donkin, and Belfast. In turn, each demonstrated his vulnerability and incompleteness. In the face of their fragility, the ship herself became veiled from them, withdrawing her protection and her certainty while they hungered. It appears that critics, like the narrative voice, hunger for a vision of this story which grants to the solidarity of the crew that bulwark against transience and meaninglessness which Conrad described so movingly in the final paragraphs. So even a critic sensitive to the underlying concerns about imperialism in the story, such as Benita Parry, continues to see the tale as one in which the sea and the land are opposed to one another, the sea, like the ship, female and transcendent in opposition to the land, which harbours class struggle 'and [where] the influence of libertarian ideas reach[es] out to threaten the hierarchy still intact in the community of the sea.'3 Again, like the affirmation of community unsupported by the text, this vision of the opposition of sea and land vanishes in the concluding pages of the narrative. What the author desired, according to his famous Preface, is 'to hold up unquestioningly, without choice and without fear, the rescued fragment before all eyes in the light of a sincere mood.' And the hope which underlies that attempt is the recreation of 'that feeling of solidarity' so fleeting on the 'Narcissus', 'which binds men to each other and all mankind to the visible world' (p. x).

Once again, there is a clear disparity between the author's expressed intent and the actuality of the text. The crew's solidarity, such as it is, rests upon their common aversion to the truth of James Wait's imminent death. As long as they reject the truth of his condition, the ship, in her wisdom, founders, tacks idly, and fails to secure the wind she needs to complete the journey. If there is any clear opposition within the text it is that between the motley crew and the external world, largely characterised as female, which obeys its own immutable and exclusive laws. Conrad claims at the end of his Preface that the ultimate attempt of the work of art is 'to compel men entranced by the sight of distant goals to glance for a moment at the surrounding vision of form and colour, of sunshine and shadows; to make them pause for a look, for a sign, for a smile – such is the aim, difficult and evanescent, and reserved only for a very few to achieve' (Preface, p. xii). This sense of affection for the transient glories of the earth seems an affirmation of the values ordinarily ascribed to the female rather than the male sensibility. It is not culture, that male artefact, which Conrad extols in his Preface but rather the sentient Earth, that great Mother ship whose image concludes *The Nigger of the 'Narcissus'*. It appears that conquest of the sea, like conquest of the tribes to the East, represents male energy at its best and its worst, especially if unleavened or uncriticised by the explicit presence of articulate women. The ship and the natural world, personified as they are in *The Nigger of the 'Narcissus'*, can only suggest a critical perspective towards the imperial and patriarchal conquest; Conrad's professed aims seem to be in regular contrast to his powerful imagery. As the crew forget their 'scare', and romanticise the voyage once they have lived precariously through the terrible storm, so the narrative voice forgets the real nature of the journey, and so the author, in his Preface, recasts his story to fit a heroic artistic mould of male triumph. It is the fidelity to the moment, at the expense of the recollection in tranquillity, which the reader must search out. And this discrepancy between event and interpretation is to become the most salient aspect of the acclaimed novels and tales of the water.

With *Heart of Darkness*, Conrad turns overtly to the confrontation and analysis of Western imperialist values and practices; in this context, women from the first play a complex and apparently contradictory set of roles. It is the aunt, based on Conrad's own relation, Marguerite Porodovska, who rushes about and uses her influence to get Charlie Marlow the berth which allows him to realise his childhood ambition and go 'there!' into the heart of Africa. In her zeal to gratify her nephew's expressed need, the aunt demonstrates that fidelity to the individual above all which characterises so many of Conrad's women throughout his writing career. Rather than the abstractions to which men seem to devote themselves – Duty, Fidelity, Work, Courage – which end so often in disillusion and in a perplexing variety of failures, women seem rather to focus sharply on the individual and the specific. The male tendency to abstract and to personify characterises the author and the narrative voice no less than the male characters; the sea itself is early on described as the 'inscrutable' mistress of the seaman who is himself an abstraction. So, from the outset, the narrative provides an illustration of Conrad's analysis of a cultural and political divide. In this way of formulating thought, the role of women – or woman – serves to further and to compensate for the nature of men – or man. As Marlow notes early on, using for the moment specific language, 'the conquest of the earth, which mostly means the taking it away from those who have a different complexion or slightly flatter noses than ourselves, is not a pretty thing when you look into it too much. What redeems it is the idea only' (*Heart of Darkness*, p. 51). Against this partial redemption one may insist that 'to burn a man is not to defend a doctrine, it is to burn a man.'[4] Characteristically, Marlow comes to a hesitant and inconclusive halt to his musings about the redemptive idea when he begins to articulate the specific image of human sacrifice. The immediate, the concrete and the tactile, often recognised and defended by the women in these texts, reproach and deny the abstractions of conquest and appropriation. Marianna Torgovnick's recent discussion of *Heart of Darkness*, in Chapter 7 of *Gone Primitive: Savage Intellects, Modern Lives*, begins the analysis of the text with a candid disclaimer: 'I have read *Heart of Darkness* many times and always been a bit repelled by it'.[5] It is, she thinks, something of the 'vagueness', the abstraction, of Marlow's style that accounts for the repulsion.

' "I don't want to bother you much with what happened to me personally" ', Marlow begins by saying, when it is what happened to him personally which must finally be what the story is about. The denigration of the 'personal' as the proper subject for great literature haunts Conrad as it has haunted male and female writers for generations. Disparagement of novelists as 'scribblers' expresses in a convenient code resentment of women writers and readers who look to literature for a meaningful presentation and analysis of the intimate terms of their lives. Looking as he did for acceptance as a great writer, Conrad struggled regularly against his tendency to explore his personal history. So Marlow's tone in the opening pages of *Heart of Darkness* subtly disparages and diminishes the meaning of the blank spot on the map, the desire to find personal meaning in the journey. In the crucial early paragraphs of *Heart of Darkness*, with their specific references to the known events of Conrad's own childhood, Marlow applies to himself images of silliness and trivialises his deep longing for travel to the heart of Africa. His compulsive need he describes as a 'hankering', and his hungry self he diminishes to the shape of 'a silly little bird.'

This need to disparage the personal and the specific nature of experience shapes much of the prose style of *Heart of Darkness* and accounts for some of its peculiar tension. The attribution of meaning to small gestures evokes from Conrad writing of a portentousness which testifies to his own uneasy ambivalence. The females in the outer office in Brussels, those black-clad and fateful creatures, see and understand all the implications of the business of imperial trade and colonisation. But that language cannot be simply expressed, for that might suggest the better understanding of women. Marlow, therefore, attributes to the women a status analogous to that of the Greek fates who knit placidly outside the gates of Hades.[6] His own aunt, Marlow asserts, represents legions of women who must be protected from the reality of the 'confounded fact' which might destroy their beautiful world of unreality. Marlow suggests that women are especially susceptible to idealistic claims because they do not encounter 'facts' as men do. Yet the text of *Heart of Darkness* illustrates something quite different. Men, Marlow among them, cling to the 'idea' in the face of the 'facts' because the facts contradict the idea entirely. *Heart of Darkness*, like *The Nigger of the 'Narcissus'*, shows the narrator determined to wrest meaning from experience even at the expense of lying about it, protecting women from the truth of the culture which imprisons them all.

Modern feminist critics disagree about the treatment of women at the hands of male novelists; the majority assert, as Nina Auerbach describes their practice, that 'men mutilate their heroines to suit their own myopic needs,'[7] but some feminist critics contribute another perspective. Auerbach herself suggests that we need to expand the focus of feminist criticism to include the study of male authors who sometimes create for their female characters 'a faith in growth, freedom, and fun, of which women's worlds, in literature at any rate, are in general sadly deprived.'[7] *Heart of Darkness* contains several kinds of women, several kinds of perspectives, testifying to Conrad's unfixed, even conflicting sense of what roles women must play both in his fiction and in the world of imperialism which is his subject.

In some respects, the enigmatic women who serve as the gatekeepers of the company office in Brussels offer the most schematic view of women as mythic powers, at home in a world deeper and more permanent than the crowded and competitive marketplace in which Charlie Marlow competes for his livelihood. Their profound understanding expresses itself through their silent manipulation of the forms of business; though 'plain as an umbrella-cover' in dress, each woman 'seemed to know all about them and about me too. . . . She seemed uncanny and fateful' (op. cit., p. 57). Yet, within two pages of text, Marlow breezily comments, 'It's queer how out of touch women are. They live in a world of their own, and there has never been anything like it, and never can be' (op. cit., p. 59). This abrupt contradiction has usually been ignored by Conradian critics. Marlow's unrepentant and uninstructed denial of women's reality (which is regularly quoted by critics) makes him a visibly inconsistent and untrustworthy reporter about individual women or women as a sex. Intimidated by the blackgarbed guardians of the company office, he patronises his aunt quite unreflectingly, and he goes on to patronise the magnificent black mistress of Kurtz as well as Kurtz's Intended. Gayatri Chakravorty Spivak cautions contemporary feminist literary critics to beware of our own tendency to 'perform the lie of constituting a truth of global sisterhood'[9] as we read, an injunction of importance in any analysis of *Heart of Darkness*. Torgovnick, in her study, assumes just such knowledge, attributing to Kurtz's black mistress a psychology which the text itself fails to assert. Torgovnick assumes, as well, the death of the black mistress, when the story remains silent in the face of her extravagant mourning and gives no hint of her end.

Spivak illustrates the imperialist male reduction of women's identity by quoting from a poem by Baudelaire, 'Le Cygne', which concludes with a listing of nameless people: 'there stands a nameless woman moving her feet in the mud, who is distinguished by nothing but colour, a derisive name for her ethnicity: "Je pense à la négresse." '[10] That black woman might well be the subject of Kurtz's painting, in *Heart of Darkness*, a black woman 'draped and blindfolded, carrying a lighted torch. The background was sombre – almost black. The movement of the woman was stately, and the effect of the torch-light on the face was sinister' (op. cit., p. 79). Even more closely, Kurtz's native mistress, as described by Marlow, resembles in her savage abstraction the 'négresse' who preoccupies Baudelaire. For Marlow, the sight is 'a wild and gorgeous apparition of a woman. . . . She was savage and superb, wild-eyed and magnificent; there was something ominous and stately in her deliberate progress.' Like Baudelaire, though in a less compressed fashion, Conrad's narrator attempts to express his vision of female savagery and the core of Africa in one elaborate image. Spivak warns us, in her analysis of Baudelaire and Kipling, among others, that we must neither accept the author's reduction of women's experience to the evocative image nor indulge our own fantasy of sisterhood with the source of the image. That is, the reader cannot, any more than Marlow could, penetrate the reality and the selfhood of that apparition across the river from Charlie Marlow. The narrative provides no opportunity for Marlow to calculate the intrinsic meaning of the black woman. The contemporary reader who now wishes to stand on the other side of the river and look from the perspective of the native woman has a position of some narrow dignity from which to observe. At the same time, as Spivak warns, we have no licence to imagine ourselves in imaginative league with the superb savage. No less than Marlow, contemporary women readers of Conrad's *Heart of Darkness* must examine their distance from the women of the text. What Torgovnick describes as a woman who seems to 'need and want no protection . . . outside, somehow, of the novella's concept of womanhood',[11] is in fact a scrupulous characterisation which preserves the separate dignity and existence of the character. And, with Marlow, women readers must face the temptation to devalue the strength, the integrity, and the willingness to know the truth about imperialism that colour the final encounter with a woman in this story: Marlow's meeting with the Intended.

Virtually all criticism concerned with *Heart of Darkness* attempts to exonerate or explain away Marlow's lie to the Intended – not because it diminishes her but because, as Marlow worries, such a lie suggests his failure to live up to the ferocious example of Kurtz, to the man who faces the ultimate truth about himself and his relation to the universe. Marlow's concern is to do 'justice' to Kurtz, and his halting conversation with Kurtz's Intended serves primarily to expose her insularity and idealisation of her lover. With increasing sarcasm, Marlow echoes and encourages her adulation of Kurtz until he speaks out of a 'dull anger' and finds himself confronted by her desperate request for Kurtz's last words.

What needs explaining in that last secton of the tale is not so much the technical lie to the Intended, the substitution of her name for 'the horror, the horror', but Marlow's sardonic and manipulative treatment of the woman from the first moments of their meeting. Indeed, Marlow's barely concealed hostility arises as the Intended ascribes to him love and friendship towards Kurtz. ' "He drew men towards him by what was best in them" ', she says. ' "It is the gift of the great." ' At this point, as at others in the scene, Marlow answers only obliquely; but his obliquity extends to his listeners as well as to Kurtz's Intended. For what this woman seems to penetrate, in her own darkness, is Marlow's weakness, Marlow's susceptibility to her own form of

adulation. It is part of Marlow's own fatal need for
abstraction and depersonalisation which allows him to
imagine for a moment the figure of the superb black woman
extending her arms as the Intended extends hers; there can
be no better rejection of the Intended's individuality than
this momentary fusing of the two images into one yearning
Woman. Paradoxically, of course, the two women share a
kind of victimisation which the framework of the tale allows
but does not discuss. They have both been shaped by the
patriarchal culture of imperialism which creates men like
Kurtz and Marlow to be esteemed and adored by such
women, all of whom will in the end be abandoned.

In his retaliatory manipulation of the conversation with
Kurtz's Intended, Marlow brings to a rounded conclusion his
attitudes towards women which have in many ways helped to
determine his behaviour throughout this complex narrative.
A man of anxious idealisation, one who finds it difficult to be
indebted to a woman, given to the deprecation of the
personal, Marlow from the outset wrestles with the provoca-
tions of women. Whether as emblems of material or sexual
power, the women of this story, seen through the language
of the narrator, emerge as larger than life. Marlow, both the
tool of imperialism and its maker, fails to comprehend the
humanity of any woman; in the end, furious with himself, he
takes refuge in indirection and duplicity to preserve the
ignorance of another powerful female figure. By lying to the
Intended, Marlow may establish the truth of his assertion
that 'women are out of touch with truth.' In his complicity
with the memory of Kurtz – whom even then he may have
failed – Marlow acts to confirm his own view of the world by
preserving the prison of imperialism for both the savage and
the Western woman. For the feminist reader of this tale,
reading from a position of detachment allows an understanding of Marlow's manipulative behaviour and defies the
invitation of the narrative to disparage the Intended along
with Marlow. Spivak's cautionary remarks about the
temptation of global sisterhood remind us that these
incompletely imagined women serve as powerful rebukes to
the glamour of the imperialist vision. They are part of the
gritty reality which is finally incapable of being redeemed

by 'the idea'. Even the wealthy woman in her shadowed drawing room for whose benefit, supposedly, the entire imperial edifice has been constructed, suffers at the hands of the agent of colonisation. Inevitably, the modern reader wonders whether one must read against the text in order to identify the real interests of the significant and disturbing women characters; the relationship between Conrad and his famous narrator, Marlow, can only be described as problematic. But it is true of all the great tales of this period that narrative tension pervades the texts. Ambiguity and ambivalence find expression in the alternation of closeness, identity, and distance between the author and the teller. From the we/they alternation of *The Nigger of the 'Narcissus'* to the creation of Charlie Marlow, Conrad displays his own uncertainty about his final implication within any perspective. Unlike Baudelaire, who impaled his own dark abstraction in one image, Conrad struggled to reform and revision his own early experiences in the Congo and in the East, brooding over his narrator even as his narrator broods over his tale. So powerful and compelling are the women who mark the story, so immense the female symbols of the ship and the earth, that the tales testify to a preoccupation on the author's part which manifests itself with or without his conscious intention.

Lord Jim, published in 1900, marks the apotheosis of Marlow as the narrator of the Conradian novel. As in *Heart of Darkness*, Marlow expresses his preoccupation with self-definition as he struggles to comprehend the figure and the meaning of Jim. As he does so often in his Author's Prefaces, Conrad takes issue with the critical remarks of a nameless 'lady' who failed to appreciate his book. In this case, Conrad notes that a lady expressed dislike of *Lord Jim*; 'but what surprised me', he notes, 'was the ground of her dislike. "You know", she said, "it is all so morbid" ' (1917 Preface, p. ix). Not only does Conrad dismiss the idea of morbidity as attached to *Lord Jim*, but in the end he dismisses the idea of the critic being European at all, thus presumably discrediting the sensibilities of such a critic. The testiness Conrad displays, seventeen years after the novel's original publication, testifies to an emotional investment comparable at the very least to Marlow's repeated assertion that Jim was 'one of us.'

In what sense might this book be legitimately criticised as morbid? And what does Conrad tell us about his vision of a woman's response to his work, in ascribing such a verdict to a woman whom he then labours to discredit? In some fashion, Lord Jim anticipates the most recent developments of critical and political theory, for it illustrates the partial, fragmentary, and necessarily incomplete visions of reality which have come to challenge earlier assertions of universality. The morbidity asserted by the nameless woman reader about Lord Jim evoked from Conrad an outraged assertion that, after all, Jim is 'one of us.' Conrad took refuge, then, in the beleaguered camp of universal meaning, a camp even then under siege. Typically, the critical attack, as Conrad describes it, comes from a woman who presumably can never be 'one of us'; yet the narrative itself concludes in failure, or at the very least without demonstrable success, in capturing Jim for the safety of British values. As he did in his earlier books, Conrad wrote in fealty to his narrative instincts and then, years later, recast his accomplishment in his Author's Preface, describing it as he needed to sustain his projection of himself.

Lord Jim concerns the dereliction from duty of a young, white merchant officer and his subsequent opportunity to redeem himself as the Tuan Jim of Patusan. In the book's alternation of points of view, and its steady scrutiny of the mutual inconsistency of fixed claims of morality, it provides a devastating critique of universality. Feminist analysis of Western patriarchy demonstrates the fallacious nature of 'universal law' which has been for generations merely a way of describing a dominant masculine set of values and hierarchies. It is precisely such universality that Lord Jim examines, perhaps, as Conrad hoped, to sustain a commitment to a code of behaviour already shown in Heart of Darkness to be inadequate. Kurtz, in Heart of Darkness, and Jim in Lord Jim may be said to be the extremes of the idea of imperialism which challenges Marlow's conception of himself and a universal ethic of behaviour. Kurtz was intended to be imperialism's finest flower, the epitome of

European civilisation, tested and found wanting – if redeemed to some extent by the authentic intensity of his experience. Jim, on the other hand, is no intellectual; he may be, in Stein's word, a romantic but he is one by instinct rather than by theoretical conviction. The sound code of ethics for which Marlow searches must, if it exists, manifest itself despite the incoherence of its practitioners. A facile speaker, as *Heart of Darkness* demonstrates, is no guarantee of the ultimate strength of the ethical vision. The nature of that vision has been recently examined by Carol Gilligan, a psychologist, in her analysis of the formation of ethical standards by men and women, *In a Different Voice*. Lawrence Kulberg, the pioneering psychologist who first developed the theory of the hierarchy of ethical visions as a developmental model, essentially described the theoretical model with which Conrad worked as a novelist. It is a model which provides for moral development in the individual on which society can depend. It is the model which provides for each individual acting as 'one of us' at the critical moment. But, as Gilligan demonstrates in her study, Western women and girls may subscribe to another model entirely, equally compelling and complete. The universal moral code in its reassuring solidarity wavers and disappears before this alternative model whose primary ethic is one of relationship rather than individual ethical honour.

Marlow's emotional and intellectual investment in Jim determines much of the formal structure of the novel. As Jacques Darras among other critics has noted, 'It is the complexity of the narration itself, and the diverse perspectives which it opens, which allow the reader to make his own judgments.' The feminist reader notes the formal structure which encourages dissent. Darras continues: 'We must always bear in mind that Marlow, however attractive his point of view may be and no matter how poetically expressed, is a hagiographer writing the life of a "saint".'[12]

Clinging to the ethical model which gives meaning to his life, Marlow searches for the heroic in Jim in the same way in which the Marlow of *Heart of Darkness* identified with Kurtz. As they did in *Heart of Darkness*, women's presences in *Lord Jim* pierce the ethical and rhetorical papier mâché which shields Marlow from the reality of genuinely altruistic behaviour. It is the presence of Jim's lover, Jewel, and her empathy with her dying mother, which takes the novel to a new level of style, one which some critics have resisted and resented. As Thomas Moser illustrates, critics often discern in what they perceive to be the 'weak portions' of even the finest novels the effects of women's intrusion. Jewel, in *Lord Jim*, represents such an intrusive presence for many critics of the novel; she is not intrusive, however, for readers who see the novel as an exploration of the differing ethical schemes lived out by men and women in a long age of colonisation, a colonisation which includes the conquest of women by men. Jewel is a complex mixture of races and cultures. Before he meets her, Marlow approaches women in Patusan with some trepidation, beginning with the wife of Doramin whose sceptical questions about Jim prove unanswerable. 'She asked me in a pitying voice why it was that he so young had wandered from his home, coming so far, through so many dangers? Had he no household there, no kinsmen in his own country? Had he no old mother who would always remember his face? ... I was completely unprepared for this' (*Lord Jim*, p. 275). These are, of course, the questions whose answers would define Jim in perfectly damning ways. As Darras suggests, the placement of Jim in Patusan may be interpreted as the 'sacrificial offering of the guilty son by the fathers in order to ensure the continued diversion of commerce and religion and the justification of Western expansion.'[13]

There is, in fact, a family in England to remember Jim's face, always. But the opportunity to flee his disgrace, to free his family from his act, prohibits Jim from communicating with his parents who love his memory. In contrast, Jewel commits her life directly to the redemption of her mother. Given the dedication of Marlow to the cause of Jim, so patently his own ethical surrogate, Jewel's account of her commitment to the memory of her mother leaves Marlow speechless. He found his mind 'troubled ... profoundly with the passive, irremediable horror of the scene. It had the power to drive me out of my conception of existence, out of that shelter each of us makes for himself to creep under in moments of danger, as a tortoise withdraws within its shell.' For Marlow, who identifies himself so easily and so fatally with those who are recognisably 'one of us', Jewel presents a new sort of problem. 'For a moment I had a view of the world that seemed to wear a vast and dismal aspect of disorder, while in truth it is as sunny an arrangement of small conveniences as the mind of man can conceive. But still – it was only a moment. I went back into my shell directly. One *must* – don't you know? – though I seemed to have lost all my words in the chaos of dark thoughts I had contemplated for a second or two beyond the pale' (op. cit., p. 313).

This self-analysis by Marlow is critically telling. For all the pain and anxiety evoked by Jim's defection, the moral universe he inhabits is one of known and knowable configuration for Marlow. His inability to live up to his romantic conception of himself may torture Jim, but it is a kind of torture with which Marlow readily empathises, a torture he understands. The fear of failing to live up to the community's image of the hero stalks Marlow and Jim alike. Jewel's fear, by contrast, conveys chaos to Marlow, for it strikes rather at the 'sunny arrangement of small conveniences' than at the threat of individual defection or inadequacy. The story of Jewel's mother suggests that one may behave perfectly and suffer endlessly in this world of sunny conveniences. Marlow's description of the 'chaos of dark thoughts' suggests a parallel to the woman poet's question: what would happen if one woman told the truth? The answer is, the world would split open.[14] What Marlow experiences here, in Conrad's astonishing risk of his narrator's representative stance, is the splitting open of the world as he knows it.

The masculine ethical struggle centres around that creation and support of the individual man who is able to internalise and live out the commitment to integrity as it is defined by the code of the colonisers: civilised behaviour. What Marlow and the reader of *Lord Jim* confront in the story of Jewel and her mother is the underside of the behaviour of civilised men. Marlow articulates and then flees from an understanding of the world from the point of view of one who is to him – almost always – alien; both the knowledge of the world from this perspective as well as the terror of accepting its reality cause Marlow to falter and to writhe in his effort to describe and to be free of this vision. 'Our common fate', as Marlow describes it, is the fate of men then visited upon women with, as he calls it, 'a peculiar cruelty' (Lord Jim, p. 276). That peculiar cruelty, understood properly, would do more to disintegrate the bonds that link Jim to Marlow than any particular behaviour might threaten. For the world as Jewel experiences it is not a place that Marlow knows; what he fears is her perspective which shatters the web of masculine ethical responsibility he attempts to reweave with Jim at its centre.

Like the fragmentary and ill-understood women of Heart of Darkness, Jewel epitomises the combination of particular and abstract knowledge which terrifies Marlow because it seems to demand a kind of behaviour which is both spontaneous and ordered. Above all, such knowledge in a woman seems to demand an immediate ethic of compassion and individually expressed love not for 'civilisation', or for all members of the society created aboard ship, but for the individual who suffers. One is related to the suffering individual. Jim's romanticism threatens to respond to the immediacy of Jewel's need, when it is Jewel's condition and the nature of her story which so disturb Marlow and leave him speechless and terrified. Jim, never articulate, stammers incoherently when trying to express what he feels for Jewel and what he owes to her. ' "You know – this – no confounded nonsense about it – can't tell you how much I owe to her – and so – you understand – I – exactly as if . . ." ' (op. cit., p. 278). Jim's incoherence, always frustrating to Marlow's desire to hear and to know the meaning of his life, is particularly noteworthy in the sections about Jewel. Ordinarily, Marlow has a construct which enables him, however superficially or incorrectly, to tell himself the tale and the meaning of the tale that Jim embodies but cannot speak. With Jewel, however, the tale is one that Marlow doesn't know and fears hearing. In the same way in which he attempted subtly to discredit the human level of knowing of the guardians of the company office in Brussels, Marlow in Lord Jim attributes to Jewel a monstrous, unnatural mode of being: the quality of a blind monster, a sphinx. 'She had no conception of anything', Marlow tells himself and his listeners. 'What notions she may have formed of the outside world is to me inconceivable: all that she knew of its inhabitants were a betrayed woman and a sinister pantaloon.' Still trying to belittle her intuition of the world, Marlow scoffs: 'I believe she supposed I could with a word whisk Jim out of her very arms; it is my sober conviction she went through agonies of apprehension during my long talks with Jim' (op. cit., p. 308).

Marlow dissimulates here; indeed, Jewel had every reason to fear the effect of Marlow upon her lover. There is a word that Marlow could say, as he well knows, which could change Jim's life. He could answer affirmatively when Jim asks whether, even now, Marlow would care to have Jim carrying out his orders aboard ship. It is that question which Marlow shies away from answering during this last visit to Jim in Patusan, and Jewel is entirely correct in her sense of the power Marlow has over Jim and thus over her life. Lying to women, by overt and covert uses of language, characterises Marlow's behaviour in *Lord Jim*, finally, just as it does in the much-analysed conclusion of *Heart of Darkness*, and for the same sort of reason: a determination not to allow the woman who loves the imperialist explorer the empowerment of knowledge. Denial of knowledge is at the heart of Marlow's protestations, evasions, and lies to women: Marlow wishes to deny to women their reality and their tenure in the real world of white men. But in order to accomplish such denial Marlow finds that he must regularly deny the reality of each such woman, ascribe to her a sort of existence which is, as he earlier suggested, 'an extra-terrestrial touch', or, as he claimed in his earlier characterisation of his aunt, 'out of it', uncontaminated but also unnourished by the grit of everyday facts and realities.

Yet, persistently, the narratives in which Marlow figures allow women precisely the kind of gritty knowledge and experience which Marlow attempts to deny them. And Jewel is perhaps the most extended example of a woman whose experience, while reducing Marlow to dismayed silence, illustrates her unflinching knowledge of the inclusive world which holds more than conquerors. Jewel's simple statement to Marlow, a statement which opens the doors to horror for him, is merely: ' "I didn't want to die weeping" ' (op. cit., p. 312). In a room with her dying mother, Jewel comes to her maturity: responding to her mother's silent entreaty to bar the door to her abusive husband, Jewel finds the strength of body and mind to act on behalf of another and to learn from her action. What Jewel illustrates is that ability to translate compassionate knowledge into immediate action. Unlike Jim (or Marlow) Jewel does not have to face the paralysis of will which seems to characterise the intellectualising romantic hero. In the moment in which she apprehends danger and distress, Jewel behaves with power and authenticity. No wonder that she fills Marlow with bewilderment, for she invalidates the long and tortured quest for meaning which he carries out on behalf of members of his class.

Towards Jim, as well, Jewel illustrates this clarity of emotion and action: from the first, she stays awake to watch over him when he is too self-absorbed to perceive his own danger. It is with some exasperation that she finally confronts him with his need to act and her own history of concern for his safety. This ability to behave decisively while in the grip of strong emotion demonstrates Jewel's hardiness and shows, as well, the self-serving falseness of Marlow's vision of women. Not 'out of it', but rather in control of the moment, Jewel acts for Jim's safety, determined not to be a passive victim of brutality as her mother had been – to the moment of her own death.

Marlow's inadequate response to Jewel, a misunderstanding equivalent to that of outsiders who mistake her valid reality as a woman for the totemic reality of a precious stone, testifies to his limitations as a narrator and warns us, if we still need warning, not to confuse him with the author. For Marlow's investment in Jim is never more apparent than in his hesitation in appraising and admiring Jewel. Casting about for solid ground, in the face of the ethical darkness which Jewel's vision of the universe suggests, Marlow falls back on the universal nature of morality, the ethical norm professed so touchingly (and so inadequately) by Jim's father in the letter which Jim carries to the end of his life. 'Virtue is one over the world', the letter states, 'and there is only one faith, one conceivable conduct of life, one manner of dying. ... Therefore resolve fixedly never, through any possible motives, to do anything which you believe to be wrong' (op. cit., pp. 341–2). The compelling nature of this faith in a universal moral code shows in Jim's having carried the letter in his wallet every day of his life. Its inapplicability to the sort of moral blackness communicated by Jewel seems clear.

A recent philosophical discussion of the conflict between the Kantian categorical imperative and a more relation-centred feminist ethical code suggests the nature of the conflict which Jewel brings to the last stages of *Lord Jim*. A letter to Immanuel Kant from Maria von Herbert, an aspiring ethicist, contains the line: 'I read the Metaphysic of Morals and the Categorical Imperative and it doesn't help me a bit.' The author of the recent analysis, Beverley Brown, notes that before one can behave in a truly charitable way, and before one can perceive each person as a subject, one must be able to understand the nature of another's place, or context. 'In order to put himself in her place he must know what that place is and address it as *different* from his own. In order to treat people as subjects it is perhaps necessary to have the intelligence to treat them as objects.'[15] This ability to enter the context of another and then to retain the knowledge in the search for ethical justice is what Marlow displays in his search for Jim but recoils from in his encounter with Jewel. The condition of women in *Lord Jim* thus remains to the end an irritant which rubs raw the gleaming inevitability of Jim's presumably redemptive death.

Uncontaminated by the mentality which continually attempts to draw back and abstract from the particular case, Jewel remains unsatisfied by Jim's enigmatic self-sacrifice. The conflict between a patriarchal, ordered universe in which individual justice can be inferred, and a woman-centred world in which chaos attends the individual life and only the particular is fully meaningful, continues to the end in this series of texts. Conrad relies on the conception of

Marlow to solve pressing problems of narration and point of view. At the same time, he uses Marlow, exposes Marlow, to allow alternative visions of reality to speak against patriarchy and colonialism. Through Marlow's incoherence and inadequacy, Conrad encourages the reader to perceive the authenticity of the individual woman's action in the world and conception of the world. Without powerful rhetoric or self-conscious posing, women such as Jewel, images such as the ship and the land, testify to an alternative principle of experience. The immense journeys of Marlow and Kurtz lead them to levels of insight which it appears women have known for some time. In some of the shorter tales, less esteemed and studied than these important novels, Conrad explored the landscape of the abyss that was familiar terrain to some of his most formidable women.

CHAPTER THREE

Some Short Stories

Conrad's short fiction has received relatively little attention from important critics. Conrad himself seems to have regarded most of his short stories as fillers, attempts, on occasion, to generate cash of which he was always in need. Frederick R. Karl's assessment is typical: 'Except for a few later efforts such as "Il Conde" and "The Secret Sharer", and, perhaps, "The Planter of Malata", Conrad's shorter fiction was not to be particularly distinguished. . . .'[1] A select few of Conrad's short stories have interested critics; apart from 'Youth' and 'The Secret Sharer', most notably these have included 'Amy Foster' and 'The Return', both of which have been read as autobiographical references to Conrad's anxieties and misgivings about marriage. Albert J. Guerard is most outspoken in his attribution of autobiographical revelation to 'Amy Foster', but other critics such as Thomas Moser and Roger Tennant take a similar approach.

Several of the short stories and tales, however, read from a feminist perspective, not only take on new meaning but new value as literary structures. For in them, it seems, Conrad explored risky ideas and sentiments which found fuller expression in the more widely recognised works, though even there, it seems, his identification with the needs and perspectives of female reality was not to be well understood.

'Gaspar Ruiz', for example, written shortly after Conrad finished the manuscript of *Nostromo*, is a story which receives little serious attention. Even in the Introduction to

A Set of Six, the collection in which the story appears, Conrad himself describes it almost entirely in terms of its narrative point of view. He is defensive about the episode which concludes Ruiz's life, in which he takes the place of an emplacement for a gun and dies of internal injuries. Certainly there is no reference to the stunning portrait of a determined woman which is at the heart of the story. The use of the general to tell the story, which Conrad credits for the 'air of actuality' which he finds in the narrative, serves as yet another masculine framing device against which and through which the voice of the woman makes itself heard. The self-absorbed male narrator, a vital element in Conrad's long fiction, often serves to illuminate both the plight of female characters and their powerful effects in the world, as much through the narrator's bewildered response as through the women's actions and characteristics.

'Gaspar Ruiz' purports to be about a strong man whose strength of body is not matched by intelligence or political sophistication. Characterised by devotion and loyalty to those who seem to care about him, Ruiz becomes the husband of a proud and passionate woman from a royalist family. In the telling of the story, the narrator indicates that only the desire to use Ruiz against her political enemies explains the woman's commitment to him. Quoting the authority of a Scottish doctor (presumably a man of dour common sense) 'with much shrewdness and philosophy in his character', the narrator ascribes to the woman superhuman character and determination of an insidious and threatening kind: 'I would say that she poured half of her vengeful soul into the strong clay of that man, as you may pour intoxication, madness, poison into an empty cup' ('Gaspar Ruiz', p. 52).

The insistence on ascribing to Ruiz only brute strength, and to his wife only diabolical motives of revenge, seems to succeed in creating a relationship of manipulation and insincerity. Yet through the narrator's words another reality insists on being heard. Gaspar Ruiz and his wife have a daughter for whose christening Ruiz brings a priest eighty miles into the interior, behind the lines of the fighting between republicans and royalists. The general notes dryly that 'to celebrate the event, I suppose, Ruiz executed one or two brilliant forays clear away at the rear of our forces, and defeated the detachments sent out to cut off his retreat' (op. cit., p. 53). The disparagement of the domestic relation which suffuses this story certainly corresponds to the tone of virtually all Conradian critics who study and comment upon Conrad's relationship with his wife, Jessie. Discussions of that marriage, like the narrator's observations about Ruiz's marriage, focus on elements of pragmatism and manipulation. The effect is, on one level, to diminish and disparage Ruiz's heroism, while attributing all the intellectual and emotional energy to a depraved and manipulative woman whose wearing of a sword 'beating upon her thigh' suggests a frustrated male trapped in a female body.

This narrative attitude, however, which blandly and persistently discredits and disparages the long affection between Ruiz and his passionate wife, eventually suggests another reality entirely. The parallel to Conrad's relationship with his wife, Jessie, seems apt here. As in 'Gaspar Ruiz', there is no word between husband and wife to suggest that they perceive their relationship as the critics describe it. Rather, all the reported evidence may be seen to attest to deep, reciprocal feeling, sustained over time and against adversity. As the story develops, and the relationship endures, the narrator's descriptions become ever more exasperated and self-serving. The general, whose narrative Conrad himself describes as vital to the peculiar success of the story, indicates early on that he was himself attracted to the woman Ruiz came to marry. Although the general is at pains, early in the narrative, to explain his commitment to a young woman of impeccable republican beliefs, he acknowledges the attraction of the enigmatic royalist woman: 'I could not help noticing her on the rare occasions when with the front door open she stood in the porch' (op. cit., p. 23). It is the passionate beauty and intensity of the young woman which attracts the general; his way of accounting for her effect is to allow to women, in times of urgency and unrest, transcendence of their usual limitations and constraints. 'If we are all brothers', the general remarks with a twinkle, 'all the women are not our sisters' (op. cit., p. 26). The meaning of this remark is at least twofold. For one, men are attracted to some women, who must then not be their sisters. For another, there is that in women which differentiates them from men in a way which goes beyond common gender differences. Under some circumstances, women acquire or achieve a kind of being which is altogether different from that of common humanity, or men. 'One of the guests observed that he had never met a woman yet who was not capable of turning out quite exceptional under circumstances that would engage her feelings strongly. "That sort of superiority in recklessness they have over us", he concluded, "makes of them the more interesting half of mankind" ' (op. cit., p. 25).

This line of discussion is in many ways reminiscent of *Heart of Darkness* and *Lord Jim*, texts in which Marlow muses from time to time about the essential difference between men and women, professing at once certainty and bewilderment. Here, in 'Gaspar Ruiz', written close to *Nostromo* which is an extended testament to women's power, authority, political understanding and charity, the meandering thoughts of the military men reveal their glib superficiality. The reader must look for opportunities to encounter the enigmatic royalist woman freed from the meshes of male text. In the early stages of the text, this is not easy, except by indirection. For the general speaks out of a lifetime of authority and self-satisfaction; his regrets consist of recollections of inexperience and innocence rather than explorations of political and personal bias which always prevent him from apprehending the reality of the other, especially when the other is a woman. 'The heat of passionate convictions, passing into hatred, removes the restraints of honour and humanity from many men and of delicacy and fear from some women. These last, when once they throw off the timidity and reserve of their sex, become by the vivacity of their intelligence and the violence of their merciless resentment more dangerous than so many armed giants' (op. cit., p. 24).

Women in this personification are creatures of passion and power, to be sure, but passions and power not defined, as are those of men, by honour and humanity. Yet moments later, in the text, the general describes the two women of the royalist household providing food, shelter and aid to the gravely wounded Ruiz with no hope of gain, in a time of near starvation for themselves. Surely such behaviour testifies to both honour and humanity on their part. Such discrepancies between theory and action typify the accounts of women provided by self-absorbed male narrators in Conrad's work, both short and long.

Within the story, the direct apprehension of Dona Erminia comes in her conversation with Ruiz while he recovers from his wounds at the hands of the republicans. Her murmured comment that, 'if she were a man, she would consider no life worthless which held the possibility of revenge', suggests her intensity and her introspection (op. cit., p. 30). Her political grasp exceeds that of Ruiz, who is preoccupied with his personal honour. As Erminia seeks to lead Ruiz to a vision of revenge beyond the immediate gratification of the insulted male, the narration portrays the full force of Dona Erminia's nature: 'The power of her will to be understood was so strong that it kindled in him the intelligence of unexpressed things' (op. cit., p. 31). This moment is critical both to the development of this tale and to the understanding of what Conrad expresses about the real power of women. It is not, as the general and other deluded male narrators suggest, that such women use men and manipulate them to express and fulfil cruel and rapacious desires otherwise festering within powerless women. Rather, the questing intelligence of the woman brings into being, or evokes, a previously unsuspected and unknown intelligence within the chosen man. This account is more optimistic, of course, than the version of the general which attributes to the woman, as do all such accounts, diabolical scheming and an intelligence driven by the need for revenge and control. But even within the framework of 'Gaspar Ruiz', women emerge from time to time in a quiet, heroic mode reminiscent of Emilia Gould and Antonia Avellanos in *Nostromo*, helping the populace recover from an earthquake, tending the victims of hardship and warfare.

'Gaspar Ruiz' is in part an extended meditation on the

ways in which women, denied straightforward legitimacy as rounded personalities, find the means of expressing themselves through disguise and indirection. In these disguises, women can count on the blindness and delusion of men: Dona Erminia, dressed like a man in poncho and hat, easily passes for a man under the gaze of the general who tells the story. The 'boy' who presses a folded letter into the palm of a sentry may be Dona Erminia as well: the sentry, specifically described as lost in thoughts of his girl, is blind to the reality that thrusts itself at him, as are the other men in the story. Such persistent narrative details themselves seem to demand a feminist reading of the story, suggesting, as they do, a subtext which informs the tale of a woman's reality so pressing that even the 'official' narrator cannot resist calling attention to it. The general, for example, as he describes the presence of the 'short fellow in a ponchc and a big hat', describes himself as wondering 'stupidly' who might have obtained the confidence of Ruiz. The narrator's stupidity is precisely the device which first obscures and then illuminates the reality of Dona Erminia. So the disguises of the characters are, in a sense, the disguises of the text: they are meant to be seen through by the 'reader' who thus becomes a teller of the real story. Ruiz himself, asked by the narrator 'what became of Dona Erminia' replies that he 'prefer[s] not to think of her at all when . . . amongst you' (op. cit., p. 46).

Ruiz's reserve suggests, in this reading, the necessary separation between felt reality and its inevitable corruption and usurpation at the hands of the authoritarian story teller. For as the general appropriates the tale of Ruiz and Erminia he subjects it to his 'stupidity', which is another form of knowledge dominated by ideology rather than unbiased observation and intuition. The struggle of the story teller is thus exemplified by Ruiz's situation, as he attempts to convey his nature and the reality of his relationship to a listener who is sympathetic but not empathetic.

Conrad as a writer of short tales often confronts these issues of felt reality and narrative distortion; the deluded narrator is, of course, characteristic of many of his most powerful and respected works. The connection, however, between fidelity to the natures and experiences of women and the deluded or self-satisfied narrator is particularly evident in a short story such as 'Gaspar Ruiz', otherwise considered an adventure story of dubious authenticity and literary value. The conclusion of the short story, with its inexorable movement towards the suicide of Erminia, illustrates vividly the strength inherent in the contest between text and subtext for the reader's attention. From Erminia's question: 'And will there be women there?' regarding the village, the reader knows that her concern is for the survival and nurturing of her daughter. She will certainly kill herself, having said earlier to her dying husband, ' "On all the earth I have loved nothing but you, Gaspar" ' (op. cit., p. 66). But the narrator does not anticipate her suicide and is terrified when it comes. As he tells the reader, what he fears is the abyss, 'dread of the abyss, the dread of the crags.' That space, those fierce projections, are the world in which Erminia lives and dies.

This short story, then, suggests in miniature a number of themes and attitudes which are important throughout Conrad's work: the vitality of the female presence, the interplay between text and narration, the subversion of 'male' values by the intense and prescient woman character. It is hardly necessary to examine all the short fiction in order to demonstrate the ways in which such themes achieve powerful expression. Consideration of a few stories will make evident the vitality of the short fiction and its interest for the feminist reader of our time.

'The Duel' is ordinarily of interest for its analysis of the pernicious effects of the Napoleonic era. Conrad refers to it as the attempt to render the ethos of the epoch, an attempt which at least some French readers, he notes, found marvellously successful. In fact, the story manages to render such an ethos while at the same time, in its ending, to demonstrate with great economy its anti-humanistic core. As long as D'Hubert lives only as an officer, without an attachment to a woman, the recurring duel, though a great annoyance, does not violate his sense of life and a meaningful existence. Perverse though it is, the extended duel actually provides meaning and form to an existence otherwise entirely outlined by army responsibilities. At the climax of the story, however, the love of a young woman succeeds in separating life from duel as no other human relationship could have done. D'Hubert realises, through the passionate response of his young fiancée, that he exists as a man, a humane and feeling man, rather than an exemplar of honour alone. The terms of the duel, based on a code of masculine honour and duty, virtually exclude human attachment of any private or domestic sort. Women, as well as the values and accomplishments of women, do not impinge on the code of the duel. Only the maid, at one episode of the duel, interferes in its demented but orderly progression. Though D'Hubert does not understand, the reader knows that she throws herself into the scene because she is in love with Feraud. Her fury, driven by fear and love, baffles and inconveniences D'Hubert who is still, at that time incapable of responding to any emotion outside the code according to which he has lived his entire adult life.

Women in 'The Duel' exist until the end of the tale outside the arena in which the real action seems to take place. Though the occasional woman attempts to interrupt the action, her class or her character prevents full access to the centre of the story. Until D'Hubert's sudden exposure to the effects of romantic love in his own life, a preoccupation with traditional heroic values consumes his energies. Ridicule, a lapse from the heroic posturing of the army, any departure from the officially sanctioned rules of combat and deportment, are the guiding forces in D'Hubert's life. Most upsetting to D'Hubert is truth which is grotesque and embarrassing: 'he dreaded the chaff of his comrades almost as much as the anger of his superiors' ('The Duel', p. 186). Thus the story suggests that the male world of ritualised sport and violence, often the same activity, depends on a preoccupation with shared values of appearance and hierarchy. The 'real' world, the diverse world of men and women as opposed to the world of men, contains more complex and diverse opinions and preoccupations. But such a world, though represented briefly by the surgeon who is 'amused' by the duel and by other variations in the routine of his practice, hardly impinges on the consciousness of the protagonists.

This story, echoing a practice Conrad made use of in a number of the novels, uses the characters of women to question the prevailing value system and to suggest, in their lives and in their practices, an alternative set of values. Women in this story, in the persons of the servant, D'Hubert's sister, and eventually in D'Hubert's young fiancée, serve to comment upon and to some extent invalidate the rigid and unimaginative set of practices which reward and also imprison the aristocratic males. Even Madame de Lionne, a woman of the aristocracy, understands in an intuitive fashion that the circumstances of the duel deserve to be ignored, banished from the drawing rooms of the civilised. That it is her intuition rather than, as Conrad says, 'her elegance or sensibility' illustrates the difference between the male approach to the duel and the female. An affair of 'honour', in the male view, is its own justification. This deep connection between male activity and 'honour', observed as well in 'Gaspar Ruiz', serves to illuminate again the distinct difference between the male and female approaches to life. In the name of honour, the male protagonists often sacrifice themselves (and those who love them) to practices with nothing else to recommend them.

Freedom from convention exists within the ranks of women; it is they who refuse to be bound by convention, though they may at first appear to be more nearly constrained by it. Their ability to violate convention in order to express passionate feeling consistently defines female nature, throughout the short stories from every period. This intuitive behaviour on the part of women is not confined to the short stories, of course; the question for critics of Conrad has to do with the association between women and intuition or between women and the irrational world. Recent analysis of Conrad's attitudes towards women and towards primitive societies as well suggests that Conrad acted and wrote as an imperialist in his assignment of the irrational, natural, intuitive role to women. This thesis is argued powerfully by Marianna Torgovnick in her study, *Gone Primitive: Savage intellects, modern lives*, in which Conrad is just one of several major male authors under scrutiny. Torgovnick confines her analysis to *Heart of Darkness*, with some reference to *Lord Jim*, but the approach clearly can be applied to many of the short works and longer novels as well.

In my judgement, the error that Torgovnick and other, non-feminist critics make is to attribute directly to Conrad the musings and speculations of the various narrators in Conrad stories and novels. This error of attribution is most apparent in connection with Marlow, of course. Most critics of Conrad are unable to separate Marlow from Conrad until the direct, snarling misogyny of *Chance*. But in fact Conrad uses the division between himself and his narrative voice throughout his career, and that division is certainly in evidence in the short stories, whether they are from the era of imperialist exploration or from the exploration of Western Europe and England itself.

Of the Western pieces, 'Amy Foster' and 'The Return' are the two short stories which are often read and interpreted as directly testifying to Conrad's nervousness about heterosexual love and marriage; a distinctly autobiographical aura attaches to 'Amy Foster', written as it was not long after Conrad's marriage. 'The Return', a later attempt, is generally dismissed as a failed attempt on Conrad's part to write a sophisticated tale of 'modern marriage' by one whose understanding of love and marriage was minimal at best. All these critical judgements take for granted that Conrad's own marriage must have been at best impetuous and quixotic, at worst cynical and superficial, judgements unsupported by any direct references in Conrad's conversation or letters. The short stories, then, have been read from the perspective of those convinced that they reveal fears and reflections about women and marriage which Conrad was powerless to hide when writing fiction directly focused on love and marriage.

'The Return' is a story which, when read carefully, certainly attributes to the husband, Alvan Hervey, smugness and self-satisfaction enough to have blinded him to the real nature of his wife and his marriage. But it is not a story which minimises or denies the power of heterosexual love or the willingness of women to commit themselves fully to relationship and intimacy. The 'modern' tendency to avoid

serious intimacy is deplored in the story. Almost a precursor
to *The Rescue*, this text examines the difficulties faced by a
young woman of intelligence and drive limited to marriage
as a means of expressing her self. Early in the story the
narrator notes that Hervey's wife-to-be (like many important
female characters, she is nameless) was 'intensely bored
with her home where, as if packed in a tight box, her
individuality – of which she was very conscious – had no
play' ('The Return', p. 120). Like Edith Travers in *The
Rescue*, the heroine of 'The Return' marries in search of
some means of self-realisation. The narrative tone is almost
unfailingly harsh, but particular condemnation is reserved
for Hervey who has the means of self-realisation but dis-
regards it entirely. In desperation, his wife presides over a
salon of sorts, linked in this practice to a heroine such as
Rita DeLastaola from *The Arrow of Gold*. There is, indeed, a
selection of desperately bored and frustrated women in
Conrad's texts who come closest to realising their individuality by encouraging the talents of young men of some
literary pretensions. Mrs Hervey is one of those women.

Told largely through the point of view of Alvan Hervey,
though with a current of curt cynicism exaggerated even for
Hervey, 'The Return' eventually reveals the desperation of
the wife and her willingness to face her own despair at the
cost of personal ruin. In her willingness to risk reputation
and security, in a futile attempt to escape the hold of her
materialistic and empty life, the wife resembles the vividly
described light fixture in the hallway of their home: 'on the
first-floor landing a marble woman, decently covered from
neck to instep with stone draperies, advanced a row of
lifeless toes to the edge of the pedestal, and thrust out
blindly a rigid white arm holding a cluster of lights' ('The
Return', p.123). Though the narrative regularly describes
Hervey and his wife as sharing equally in the mindless
existence which skims over the surface of life, the imagery
here suggests that the wife suffers from her imprisonment
and from the airlessness of her life. At the conclusion of the
image of the female light fixture, thrusting towards the
open air beyond the pedestal, the narrative notes that

Hervey 'had artistic tastes – at home.' The attempt to break
into the air must be made by a woman alone.

Through the narration, which is largely confined to the
sensibilities and perceptions, such as they are, of Alvan
Hervey, the reader glimpses the wife's desperation. Her
return, bedraggled, dirty, and confessional, provides a
strong contrast to Hervey's total preoccupation with appearance. A lengthy image of Hervey reflected in the pier glass
of his wife's wardrobe serves to remind the reader of
Hervey's dependence on surface and conventional reflection;
at the same time, his alienation from genuine experience
and emotion are projected relentlessly. The evidence of his
wife's letter, left for him amid the clutter of conventional
objects on his wife's dressing table, offends him because a
servant might have seen it. 'That she should leave it like
this – in evidence for chance discovery – struck him as so
outrageous that, thinking of it, he experienced suddenly a
staggering sense of insecurity, an absurd and bizarre flash
of a notion that the house had moved a little under his feet'
(op. cit., p. 125).

Hervey's sense of propriety is outraged: 'And there was
nothing but humiliation' (op. cit., p. 127). His wife's death,
he thinks, would have been infinitely preferable to her
departure with another man, especially a man whose
stature in the world is not as great as her husband's. In this
interior musing, Hervey reveals himself in the hands of the
author as self-preoccupied to a degree unusual even for most
Conradian males. By the time Hervey thinks concretely:
' "The woman's a monster, but everybody will think me a
fool" ', he has been revealed to the reader as a sort of
monster himself. Like Marlow in *Lord Jim*, Hervey experiences a moment during which he perceives the immense
moral complexity and sadness of the world (the world
ordinarily fashioned, as Marlow notes, for the comforts of
men such as himself). 'As a landscape is seen complete, and
vast, and vivid, under a flash of lightning, so he could see
disclosed in a moment all the immensity of pain that can be
contained in one short moment of human thought' (op. cit.,
p. 133). This moment is similar also to that brief period in

'Gaspar Ruiz' when the general feels himself reeling at the vision of the abyss and the crags surrounding it. In both cases, the male protagonist experiences giddiness and terror in the face of the universe as it exists for women, and he recoils immediately. In some sense, the narration of the tale is a kind of expiation for the denial of that realm of suffering. As the narrator of 'The Return' goes on to explain, the male who recoils from an agonising moment of full participation in the universe of pain takes refuge again in a life of pretence and detail, a return to 'the painful explaining away of facts, the feverish raking up of illusions, the cultivation of a fresh crop of lies' (op. cit., p. 134).

With the return to rationalisation comes the recollection that his wife had been his property but was now property no longer. The language of the stock market characterises these anguished recollections. 'He took stock of his losses.' Such feelings as those which threaten to overwhelm Hervey with a sense of his wife's sufferings describe themselves to him as 'unprofitable sentiments.' By contrast, his wife's anguish is visible and total. Making no effort to conceal or to recover from her experience, Hervey's wife abandons herself to the full physical and mental dimensions of her pain. Muddy, dishevelled, she brings the mud and the grit of the outside world into the antiseptic confines of her dressing room. Looking directly at her husband, she confronts him with 'anguish naked and unashamed, the bare pain of existence let loose upon the world' (op. cit., p. 141).

In this confrontation lies the heart of this story and that of several of the short stories and novels as well. In such a scene, Conrad presents both the capacity and the willingness of his women characters to be engaged with the world in a powerful and authentic way. Confronted by the pain and ambiguity of the universe, many Conradian male protagonists, from Marlow to Lingard, take refuge in platitudes and conventions: work, order, the code of the sea all are invoked as means of keeping the stark disinterest of the universe from unhinging the social order. But female characters such as Mrs Hervey are numerous as well. Like her, Jewel in *Lord Jim*, Emilia Gould in *Nostromo*, Aissa in

An Outcast of the Islands stare directly into the human and moral abyss which is the world.

The husband in 'The Return' expects his pain to shake the world, to change its dimensions and its appearance; he is surprised to note that nothing changes. He perceives the mute and disinterested world as the ally of his wife: 'immobility and silence pressed on him, assailed him, like two accomplices of the immovable and mute woman before his eyes' (op. cit., p. 145). It seems characteristic of the male protagonist to envision the world as reflective of his condition; the relationship between the man and the world is different in kind from that of the woman and the world. The draped female light fixture is in this sense as well emblematic of the position of the wife, of any woman: stepping forward from a precarious and convention-bound place, she thrusts herself towards a world unseen and unknowable. The expectations which the woman brings to her journey towards the world are different in kind from those which the man carries; nowhere is this difference more acute and visible than in these short stories. Where the husband looks to the world to be faithful to his needs, the wife attempts, rather, as she says, to be faithful to herself and honest to her husband. That search for an inner self which recognises the indifference of the universe is more difficult and more human than the self-righteous search for answers which characterises many male heroes. Rhetorical flourishes characterise Hervey's discourse, flourishes which belong to the character and not to the narrative voice.

The distinction between the character and the narrative voice suggests the detachment of the author, dispelling the notion that this story incorporates Conrad's own anxieties about marriage. Rather, the narrative regularly juxtaposes the self-righteous pronouncements of the husband with the brief, direct, and self-disclosing remarks of the wife. In addition, the narrative allows the wife to comment directly on the lack of any comparable level of disclosure from Hervey. 'The indelicacy of his obtuseness angered her', a felt response which allows the reader to understand the anger and repugnance experienced by the shaken woman. That revulsion comes from the visible self-absorption of the husband: 'she perceived, just in time, that being absorbed by the tragedy of his life he had absolutely forgotten her very existence' (op. cit., p. 153).

Several of the short stories, but most particularly 'The Return,' suggest strongly that a woman may be more open to the reality and indifference of the universe, less disposed to substitute a convention, even a convention such as revenge, for the authenticity of experience, than a man. 'The Return' is most explicit in proposing that a newly honest relationship is so perilous that a husband must leave rather than become engaged in such a project. After lecturing on the virtues of 'self-restraint', almost a parody of Marlow's commitment to 'restraint' and 'work' as the means of staving off anxiety and capitulation in the face of an indifferent universe, the husband in Conrad's story encounters the emptiness of his own platitudes and his own existence. In many ways, the interior monologue of Alvan Hervey suggests the thoughts that must have animated Kurtz, in *Heart of Darkness*, when he justified to himself his departure from the empty injunctions of his Western morality. For Hervey, ever more strident in his defence of convention, realises with every pronouncement his own disbelief and alienation. The interrupted and broken sentences testify to his inability to convince himself, let alone his wife, of these platitudes. The difference between morality and convention has never been so plain as in these tortured utterances. Characteristically, the wife expresses herself shortly and directly. She expresses herself as well in laughter which Hervey treats as hysterics, dashing a tumbler of water upon her, barely able to keep from throwing the tumbler itself. The impulse towards violence carries great authenticity here. Male rage in response to female behaviour unconstrained by the property relationship is intense and angry. To himself and to his wife Hervey can scarcely articulate the sources of his rage which is in fact the expression of fear. Remembering his wife's raucous laughter, Hervey knows that 'the experience, however, contemptuously he tried to think of it, had left the bewilderment of a mysterious terror.'

That terror is twofold. In part, Hervey's fear reflects the disruption of the 'property tie' which previously defined his hold over his wife and his place in the world. But in part the fear represents knowledge of a deeper disorder in the world. 'There was an utter unreserve in her aspect, an abandonment of safeguards, that ugliness of truth which can only be kept out of daily life by unremitting care for appearances' (op. cit., p. 167).

His wife has become unknown to Hervey, an unquantifiable individual of her own mysterious volition. The narrative reveals an anxiety beyond the momentary fear of exposure and loneliness in the social world. Hervey longs for 'the sight of a man's face . . .' Any man's face 'would have been a profound relief' (op. cit., p. 173). Here the text reveals the particularity of the term 'man', for Hervey quite literally longs for men to save him from the world of women. Until now, there have been women servants in the house, at the express wish of the wife. Now, Hervey thinks, he will have men servants. 'He would engage a butler as soon as possible' (op. cit., p. 173). The refuge in maleness, in the illusion of solidarity, certainty and power calls to Hervey. He feels 'impotent' in the face of his wife's stillness and inwardness, having none of his own. Her 'sincerity' frightens and appals him, contributing to his bewilderment.

Though Hervey experiences bafflement in the face of his wife's remoteness, the narrative penetrates her silence. She is filled 'with bitter resentment against both the men who could offer to the spiritual and tragic strife of her feelings nothing but the coarseness of their abominable materialism. In her anger against her own ineffectual self-deception she found hate enough for them both' (op. cit., p. 176). The narrative certainly suggests here a clear separation between Conrad and his male characters, allowing the reader to glimpse directly a woman's rage honestly directed at herself *and* at the men who disappoint her desires and hopes. It is in fact that honesty which distinguishes the wife's character here and with which feminist readers of this era can still identify. The wife recognises the degree to which she participated in her own interment in marriage. Like Edith Travers, she acknowledges her investment, again in financial imagery, in a relationship based on a social fiction. Determined to clarify her position for herself, she speaks honestly to a man unable to bear honesty. She names the self-love which is at the heart of the thoroughly conventional marriage. 'You loved yourself', she says simply to her husband, at the conclusion of a brief statement characterising their marriage as one of convenient reflection. For the reader, these penetrating lines must bring back memories of the pier glass in the dressing room, a glass which served to reflect and to refract the broken figure of Alvan Hervey, dazzled by his own company at once approaching and retreating from his gaze.

Conrad's aspirations for marriage may be deduced from the treatment he offers in this story and in others such as 'Amy Foster.' Certainly 'The Return' suggests the highest ideals for marriage rather than a cynical assessment of its possibilities. The use of marriage, for a spirited woman, as an escape from the house of the father is clearly fraught with danger and disappointment. The achievement of the female self, this tale suggests, does not come about through an escape but through a perilous venturing forth. Such a venture may be one into the world of relationship, even relationship refounded after disaster, as the marriage of the Herveys could be if Alvan Hervey were capable of such rededication. The conclusion of the story tells the reader emphatically that such a possibility does not exist: shattered by the revelations of the abyss, Hervey leaves the house, the marriage and his former life, never to return. That this constitutes cowardice on his part seems evident. His is the expression of failure and fear: every woman, even his housemaid, now seems to him to harbour fearful information about the darkness at the heart of the universe. Woman's unknown and unknowable nature threatens Hervey with the loss of faith and hope. The certain world of property and possession has changed, in this instant, into the abyss. What Hervey wants, what Conrad suggests *men* want, from women is relief from the uncertainty of the world, from uncertainty itself. What women want, the wife suggests – Conrad suggests – is *themselves*. Hervey's wife stammers in response to his demand to know: ' "I've a right – a right to – to myself" ' (op. cit., p. 185).

These demands, for knowledge and for oneself, stand in violent opposition in 'The Return' as they may be observed to stand in many of the longer texts written by Conrad. A woman's attempt to achieve selfhood, that brave and difficult venture into the unknown, often frightens and tests a man's desire for safety and certainty in a world of difficulty and challenge. Often, even in a successful love relationship such as that of Emilia and Charles Gould in *Nostromo*, or Jewel and Jim in *Lord Jim*, the woman represents a form of knowing which is protective of a man who acts bravely but feels helpless in the face of the indifferent universe. The 'abyss' often represents an experience of the world familiar to women and fearful to men. Conrad seems to suggest, here, not only differing forms of understanding but different forms of bravery, as well. Male bravery often takes the form of action designed to dispel the terrors of contemplation; by contrast, female action serves to confront such knowledge at its source: Jewel's determination 'not to die weeping', or Emilia Gould's actions to protect those dominated by the world of 'material interests' which consume her husband.

Perhaps the most graphic and unsparing examination of the difference between a male and a female experience of the mindless forces of the universe is explored in the short story 'The Idiots'. This short story has been described as one of several, including 'The Return', suffused with 'intense hostility towards women', expressed through images of rage, hatred, and murder.[2] It seems clear that critical perspective has everything to do with the analysis of such stories. From the standpoint of a feminist reading, the empathetic portraits of women's situations and their determination to understand and to act out their real alternatives testifies not to fear and hatred of women but to empathy and compassion. In these stories and novels, Conrad shows clear signs of the willingness to engage some of the great and enduring human issues of his own time and ours; not simply 'women's lot', but the connection between the lives of women and the nature of the universe serves as the central concern of such stories. It is possible, of course, if the critic works from an analysis of Conrad as fearful and hostile to women, to assign to such texts horror and loathing rather than compassion and empathy. Such a reading, however, significantly narrows any assessment of Conrad, ascribing to him the limited views of his male narrators rather than the stature of the writer of the whole tale. The author, in such a limited view, has responsibility only for the point of view of the narrator, a critical approach characteristic perhaps of naive readers but hardly of sophisticated critics. However, the view that Conrad feared women, and that he was especially fearful and troubled around the time of his marriage, permeates the work of many important Conradian critics. Such a view necessarily determines the approach to the story of 'The Idiots', the relentless account of the nature of peasant life whose emphasis has always been on the production of children to work the land and bring benefit to an entrenched system of patriarchal ownership and inheritance.

The tragedy of successive idiot children is experienced differently by their unhappy parents. The father, having married for the sake of the land, looks to each successive child for the son who will walk the rows in his turn; a daughter will bring such a young man to the farm, but she will have no such value in herself. The wife should bear such children; failing to produce healthy children serves only to make the wife vulnerable to repeated pregnancies, and it is the final approach of her single-minded husband that leads to the cataclysmic conclusion of this stark tale. Read by a reader sensitive to the events and characterisations of the story, unconvinced by accounts of Joseph Conrad's character which attribute to him crippling anxieties about women, marriage and childbirth, this story clearly depicts the crushing weight of brutal peasant life on a suffering woman. Animated by her suffering, looking for solidarity with first her husband and then her mother, Susan ultimately kills her husband and then herself. Empathy for her character and for her sufferings animates the story and touches the reader. What, then, allows a prominent critic to attribute to such a story hatred and fear of women? The assertion that

Conrad suffered grave and pervasive anxiety immediately after his marriage, leading him to project such feelings onto the characters of hostile and frightening women, falters in the face of complacent letters from Conrad describing his comfortable life. Nevertheless, Karl remains fixed in his conviction that 'The Idiots' expresses fears and rages so well that Conrad was temporarily purged of them, rather than accepting the story as a legitimate expression of a woman's suffering in the real world.

From a feminist perspective, the denial of autonomy to the female character seems charged with the critic's own reluctance to surrender a reading that represents his own power. The denial of value to Conrad's marriage has a number of critical consequences, not least of which is the attribution of repressed rage and fear to Conrad. That rage and fear is then projected by such critics onto the stories and tales which focus on hurt, angry, and powerful women, negating their struggles by attributing them to a frightened author incapable of achieving integration in his life or his work. Such a critical perspective is clearly at work in the reading of 'The Idiots' which refuses to grant to Susan her own suffering or her own understanding of its cause.

Unconvinced, and thus unhindered by such a reading of Conrad's life, one is free to experience 'The Idiots' not simply as an example of Maupassant-like realism but as a telling and brutal example of a woman's suffering in her own peasant culture. Marriage, childbirth and motherhood, experienced at their best in the service of the land, threaten to destroy Susan's sense of self entirely when she gives birth to four idiot children. It is amazing that she possesses still enough selfhood to look to her mother, finally, for solace and affirmation, after having killed her husband as he attempted to make her pregnant yet once more in hopes of a real son. It is not surprising that her mother rejects her: clinging to her own precarious position in a world which strictly defines women's rights and duties, Susan's mother wants only to keep her respectability in her old age. A moment after rejecting her daughter's anguished appeal, the mother 'as if awakened ... from a long nightmare' rushed after her daughter, but by then Susan was on her way to death. That long nightmare was, of course, the life of acceptance and self-denial which allowed the mother to become disconnected from her daughter and from her own self.

These stories suggest, from a variety of perspectives, that women experience a world which is different in kind from the world known by men. The world of women is not 'domestic' as a sphere but is rather the world of cosmic indifference and solitude known to the author and, at flickering intervals, to the male protagonists in stories and novels. Because, perhaps, of their subjectivity and the absence of illusion, women characters encounter the indifferent world directly and consistently. Their demand for honest regard, expressed through direct looks and unveiled countenances, presents a challenge to men which is rarely met with joy or confidence. Occasionally, however, as in 'The Duel', the candid gaze of a woman allows a fortunate man to enter a new realm of experience which includes love and companionship. These concerns are consistent with those of the works throughout Conrad's life. Within the shorter fiction, untroubled by the needs for development, Conrad was often able to express such visions quickly and intensely, without the ambiguity inherent in longer and more complex characterisations.

CHAPTER FOUR

A Rich Prospect

The three great novels of Conrad's middle period, *Nostromo* (1904), *The Secret Agent* (1907), and *Under Western Eyes* (1911), present a galaxy of women so powerful, so thought-provoking and so rewarding to contemplate that we must still marvel at the richness of Conrad's imagination. The dilemmas and the resolutions which the novels explore are still to a great extent those which preoccupy thoughtful men and women of our own time. The lasting effects of colonialism (*Nostromo*), the breakdown of civil life in the city (*The Secret Agent*), and the attempt to transform the nature of Russian life (*Under Western Eyes*) are certainly among the most engaging and revealing subjects which we still struggle to understand and to escape from. Like Winnie Verloc in *The Secret Agent*, we may assert that life doesn't bear much looking into; at the same time, however, like the other heroines of these great novels – Emilia Gould in *Nostromo* and Natalia Haldin in *Under Western Eyes* – we also command our courage to envisage both change and reconciliation.

Because women are so undeniably central to these novels, the task of the feminist critic changes. It is no longer necessary to tease out the presence of women or a critique of patriarchy, since both are so evident. However, the characterisations have been so persistently misunderstood, the women so regularly explained and explained away as idealistic victims of complex ironies or political machinations, that the feminist critic must rediscover the genuine characters within the pages of the novels, freed from the critical wrappings which disguise them. As Conrad stated in the Author's Note to *The Secret Agent*, the book is 'the story of Winnie Verloc . . . complete from the days of her childhood to the end . . .' though critics regularly ignore that assertion. At the end of his Author's Note Conrad says that 'telling Winnie Verloc's story to its anarchistic end of utter desolation, madness, and despair' he did not intend 'to commit a gratuitous outrage on the feelings of mankind.' The Author's Note, written some years after the publication of the book (1920) testifies to the misreading the book received from the first. That misreading of all Conrad's major works, rests on a simple set of misconceptions and notions about Conrad's own family history and his attitude towards women which must be addressed in order to leave the works free for appreciative and fair analysis based on new appreciation of the rounded presence of mature, charming women in Conrad's background and in these important works.

Zdzislaw Najder has been in recent years the most useful source of new information about Conrad's family history, providing translations of letters between Conrad's parents which reveal them, especially Conrad's mother, to have been vital, humorous, courageous people rather than the austere, gloomy, illusion-driven revolutionaries portrayed by many Conradian biographers and critics. Because critics, especially psychoanalytically-oriented ones, took their departure from historically incomplete or incorrect portraits of Ewa and Apollo Korzeniowski, their confident attributions of Conrad's attitudes towards idealistic women to his doomed mother badly need revision and new understanding. Najder provides ample evidence for a richer, fuller interpretation of the key heroines of Conrad's mature novels.

In his Author's Note to *Nostromo*, Conrad provides an autobiographical aside which focuses attention on a young woman comrade of his youth in Poland, offering her as a source for Antonia Avellanos: 'I have modelled her on my first love. . . . She had perhaps more glow and less serenity in her soul than Antonia, but she was an uncompromising Puritan of patriotism with no taint of the slightest worldliness in her thoughts' (pp. xxiii–xiv). In fact, it is not

Antonia's characterisation which has been regarded as problematical in *Nostromo*; rather, it is Emilia Gould, with her insight and her gradual loss of resilience in the face of 'material interests' who demands new understanding in relation to the facts of Conrad's biography. For the relationship between committed idealists has more to do with Conrad's parents than the serenity of Antonia Avellanos has to do with Conrad's infatuation with his schoolmate. It is mature love that critics claim Conrad could not delineate, attributing his lack to the doomed and gloomy passion between his parents. Yet the researches of Najder reveal a pair of young people committed both to one another and to their politics, strong minded and strong hearted. It is Najder who points out the positive toughness in the young Ewa who defied her family, including her beloved father, to become engaged to Apollo and wait for nine years to marry him. She was 'by all accounts everybody's favourite in the family . . . renowned for her beauty and also for her intelligence.' It seems that she also possessed an interesting and powerful combination of qualities: 'intensely loyal, deeply patriotic and religious, she commanded both respect and affection.' In addition, the young Ewa was an active co-conspirator with her husband. Evidence, in the form of reminiscences and letters, 'shows her as a spontaneous and enthusiastic ally.' Further, Najder notes, 'there is every reason to consider her marriage a very happy one; all misfortunes came from outside.'[1]

The devotion that Apollo and Ewa felt for one another took its colour and its power from their shared devotion to the cause of Polish patriotism as they understood it. Though they were both of the landed gentry, their commitment to Polish nationalism was not founded on the perpetuation of a system which exploited a class of landless peasants. Apollo was consciously devoted to 'the liberation of peasants and against capitalism, industrialism and the rule of money.' His sense of egalitarianism seems to have been similar to that which contemporary theory would call 'equality of opportunity', and it was 'grounded in the traditional ideals of fidelity, honour, patriotism, and piety.' The sort of equality that Korzeniowski advocated was deeply Christian and took for granted a concept of individual human dignity.[2] Though both of Conrad's parents may be characterised as idealistic, they were hardly thoughtless patriots. Most importantly, for readers who wish to locate the creation and function of key women characters and political analysis in a feminist tradition, the line of thought and action which Conrad's parents represent underlines and supports some of the most powerful presentations in the great middle novels. Accused by critics from Mudrick to Moser, from Baines to Meyers of an inability to imagine complex, attractive women in relationships of maturity and as individuals of stature, Conrad had in fact a model of such people and such maturity before him in his childhood and in his memory.

The early courtship and marriage of Emilia and Charles Gould, with its dedication to the living memory of Charles Gould's father and his desire to serve the cause of political and economic development while retaining moral and emotional sanity, is reminiscent of the devotion of Conrad's young parents to one another. The fervour of the attachment between the young Emilia and the young Charles surely owes much to the sense that their energies will be devoted to the accomplishment of a continuing act of large meaning. What Emilia Gould comes eventually to identify painfully as 'material interest' serves at first to glamorise Charles and his history. In the same sense, Apollo and Ewa epitomised for one another national and intellectual values which could not be separated from the personal charm which they exuded for each other. Ewa was both supportive of her husband and aware of the cost of his idealism to the world. Our contemporary feminist awareness that the personal is the political was comprehended by her concern for the behaviour of the individual landowner and the experience of the individual peasant. Like Emilia Gould, who was able to distinguish one young peasant child from another, Ewa Korzeniowska charted the course of 'current agricultural reform' in May 1861.[3] In other words, the experience of economic activity for her was not abstract; nor do the letters give any indication that the personal and the familial were of less significance than the classically political, or that they were unconnected in her mind. Exile, the inevitable out-

come of revolutionary behaviour, promised both hardship
and a sort of freedom to live out the consequences of political
commitment. Integration of public and private, theoretical
and practical, appealed to Ewa Korzeniowska; that integration is the expectation of the heroine of *Nostromo*, Emilia
Gould. The tragic dissolution of the bond between Emilia
and Charles Gould in *Nostromo* illustrates the end of an
illusion. The son of parents who lived their relationship to a
different conclusion, Conrad had every reason to recognise
both the attraction and the peril of a love based on physical,
intellectual, emotional, and political attraction.

Within the text of *Nostromo*, the most persistent characterisation of Emilia Gould comes through the perspective of
Dr Monygham, the self-condemning and ironic survivor of
torture at the hands of Guzman Bento. His view of Emilia
Gould is both devoted and distorted, for he focuses on her
gradual loss of her husband to the lure of the silver mine
and material interests. That loss is indeed heart-rendingly
portrayed. But Conrad does justice as well to the commitment to social justice exemplified by Emilia Gould's 'schools
and hospitals', so often referred to as inadequate to replace
the love of husband and children in their marriage. The
political intelligence demonstrated in the letters and reported in the behaviour of Ewa Korzeniowska is characteristic of Emilia Gould as well. Founded on a sceptical
intelligence and a willingness to focus on the specifics of
everyday life, Emilia Gould's empathy and compassion
distinguish her Sulaco experience. She inspires the same
sort of reverence that reminiscences of Ewa Korzeniowska
testify to.

Biographers and chroniclers of the life of Joseph Conrad
often comment disparagingly upon the intelligence and the
physical attractiveness of Conrad's wife, Jessie. Virtually
every critic comments on the perceived intellectual disparity, on Jessie's lack of charm and sophistication, on her
limited grasp of the abstract concepts of political and social
reality. From another perspective, one might rather value
Jessie Conrad's freedom from illusion, freedom from the
compelling desire, so wearying to Emilia Gould, so briefly
attained by Ewa Korzeniowska, to live out a relationship

with a man founded on a joint and equal political and moral commitment to social and economic justice. The attainment of a stable family structure, including the bearing and nurturing of children, appears to have seemed to Conrad to be in itself a fully demanding, even heroic, accomplishment in life. Likewise, the creation and sustenance of a relationship between men and women equally committed to affecting the life of the world outside the marriage appears to have been fully demanding in Conrad's eyes. The value judgements recorded by Conradian critics about the style and appeal of Jessie Conrad testify to a set of beliefs about the relative worth of the separate domains of the personal and the political which are not to be found in Conrad himself: not in his parents' lives, not in his own life, and not in these great central novels in which women are the political bearers of the texts. Considering the evidence that remains in the form of letters from Conrad's mother to his father, and in the powerful portraits of women in the central novels, coupled with Conrad's own long-term commitment to his wife, Jessie, the contemporary critic needs to look with fresh vision at the roles of women and domestic life in Conrad's work.

In the letters to Apollo Korzeniowski when he was in hiding, and then in the letters which she wrote while he was in prison, Ewa Korzeniowska gave expression to a fusion of emotions and thoughts which find echoes in the lives and effects of the women in the three novels of Conrad's middle career. Devoted to the concept of a career, Ewa wrote to Apollo in 1861 extolling the virtues of a working life free from hypocrisy:

> Just like you I wish you to enter into closer contact with the circles that are inaccessible to you on account of Kazimierz's absence. Just like you I wish for an appointment in some theatre management. No less than you I am prepared to renounce all the joys of life so as not to be defiled by *that* which throughout your life you have tried to shun and which until now you have not touched. . . . I shall always be happy with you.[4]

This expression of devotion, linked to the desire for a working life unmarked by bribery and influence peddling, is

surely reminiscent of the youthful anticipations of Emilia
Gould. Like Emilia, Ewa Korzeniowska empathises with
her husband's determination to have a productive and
socially valuable career free from the inevitable corruption
that impinges on the lives of other artists. Like Emilia
Gould, Ewa Korzeniowska expresses her idealism as a facet
of her confidence in her husband and in their relationship.
'She had great confidence in her husband', Conrad writes of
Emilia in the early pages of *Nostromo*: 'it had always been
very great. He had struck her imagination from the first by
his unsentimentalism, by that very quietude of mind which
she had erected in her thought for a sign of perfect competency in the business of living' (*Nostromo*, p. 50). If Elimia,
like Ewa, was mistaken in her attribution of perfect loyalty,
the fault lies as much with the world, driven by the fires of
Western capitalism, as it does with the nature of youthful
idealism. The helplessness of the critic in the face of such a
precarious relationship should find recognition in Najder's
assessment of the marriage of Conrad's parents: 'there is
every reason to consider [their] marriage a very happy one;
all misfortune came from outside.'[5]

Scepticism about the strength of even the most satisfying
personal relationship in the face of a repressive political
system or an inhumane economic environment underlies a
statement such as Najder's; it is what accounts for the force
of the observation that the personal *is* the political. A sharp
focus on the personal cost of political commitment, and a
focus on the corrosive effect on the integrity of even the most
passionate affection of imperialism and autocracy characterises all the great novels in this period of Conrad's life. In
every book it is clear that the women characters, like
Conrad's own mother, calculate and absorb the costs of
political and economic reality upon their domestic lives.
Conrad's understanding about such relationships seems to
be as subtle and as sophisticated as that of feminist analyses
of our own time. In a culture framed by and dominated by
material interests, marriage contributes to those interests
as it provides an idealised retreat for the man who daily re-
enters the world of business and competition, relinquishing
the world of culture and religion to the female, domestic

sphere. Throughout his writing career, but most particularly in these novels, Conrad displays both his awareness of this Victorian pattern and his emancipation from its constraints. It seems clear that he owes his critical vision to the relationship which early formed him, that between his strong-willed and equally committed parents. The inability of the familial hearth to preserve domestic safety, in the harsh conditions of political exile, must have contributed to an awareness that the family is part of the state, that women are co-conspirators as they are equal sufferers at the hands of an inhumane system. Thus, in *Nostromo*, the co-conspirators include both married and unmarried women, Emilia Gould and Antonia Avellanos, both at least as thoughtful in their political and economic understanding of Sulaco and Costaguana as any of the men whom they advise and love. Though male characters may patronise the intelligence of the women, their author does not. And finally, in *Under Western Eyes*, a novel in which male claims to 'feminism' receive scathing treatment from Conrad, the thoughtful and clear-sighted analyses of repression, revolution and reconciliation are all expressed and lived out by women characters who clearly command both the respect and the admiration of the author and a new generation of readers.

Not surprisingly, most criticism of *Nostromo* has focused on the imaginative construction of the country of Costaguana, the swarming life of the South American emerging republic whose experiences have seemed veritable prefigurations of events in Central and South America since *Nostromo* appeared in 1904. Critics have also marvelled over the portraits of Charles and Emilia Gould and Martin Decoud. However, there has been no proper analysis to link the political life of Sulaco to the emotional life of Emilia Gould. The world of criticism has taken for granted the separation of the private and public worlds which, in his finest efforts, Conrad portrays as inevitably fused. Both the need for and the ultimate cost of revolution are best understood, indeed epitomised, by the major women characters in *Nostromo*. At the conclusion of his Author's Note to *Nostromo*, Conrad imagines a last glimpse of Antonia Avellanos, 'a relic of the past disregarded by men awaiting impatiently the Dawn of other New Eras, the coming of more Revolutions' (p. xiv).

Conrad's own assessment in 1917 of the place of Antonia Avellanos in the engendering, the nurturing, and the mourning of the political transformation of Sulaco is a telling one, reflecting as it does not only thirteen years of additional European and South American history but the years during which Conrad articulated some of his most prescient thoughts about the connection between the domestic and the public spheres of political action. From the earliest scenes in *Nostromo*, the theme of political cost is clearly identified with feminine comprehension. From Teresa Viola to Emilia Gould, the women characters both enter and deplore the public political realm, understanding that for the men commitment to politics is inextricably involved with a sense of personal identity both irresistible and dangerous. Nostromo's susceptibility to the 'praise from strangers' which is epitomised by the meaning of his adopted name, forms part of the lament that Teresa Viola expresses: ' "*Avanti*! Yes! That is all he cares for. To be first somewhere – somehow – to be first with these English. They will be showing him to everybody. 'This is our Nostromo!' " She laughed ominously. "What a name. What is that? Nostromo? He would take a name that is properly no word from them" ' (op. cit., p. 23).

The insight into Nostromo's dependence on others for his very name is by no means uncharacteristic for Teresa or for any other major female figure in this novel. The quality of understanding regularly appears in Conrad's women characters and, indeed, allows them to communicate rapidly and subtly with one another in a kind of shorthand conversation which bypasses the more usual formal exchanges among the men. Emilia Gould's 'delicate shades of self-forgetfulness' which enable her to facilitate social and personal exchanges are only the most polished form of an intuitive mastery of self which the women share and depend upon in themselves and among themselves. Remembering the political dedication and understanding of Ewa Korzeniowska, no contemporary reader need assume a disinclination for politics on the part of women in these novels by Conrad,

or an immutable divide between the realm of the political
and the realm of the personal (or feminine). Rather, what
emerges throughout *Nostromo*, the first of the mature
political novels, is a portrayal of politics which appeals to
the elements within personalities who typify the male and
female figures. The men, virtually without exception, are
vulnerable to political action because it provides them with
identities that only seem secure. The boyishness of Charles
Gould is but one form of the arrested development which
characterises the male characters in *Nostromo*, from Dr
Monygham's self-doubt to Martin Decoud's pose of cynicism.
'Perfect competency in the business of living', the charm of
Charles Gould in the imagination of Emilia Gould, represents the performance to be expected of men in the world.
But in fact, as Conrad demonstrates repeatedly, without
introspection and self-knowledge, the male characters do
not demonstrate that perfect competency. That 'quietude of
mind' in Charles, which Emilia erects into a virtue, reflects
a lack of self-scrutiny desirable perhaps in a man of action
but ultimately responsible for a failure of personal integration at the highest level.

On occasion, and even within Nostromo, Conrad provides
an example of the fusion of masculine energy and feminine
self-knowledge within the political realm, despite his narrative disdain for such a fusion. 'A woman's true tenderness,
like the true virility of man, is expressed in action of a
conquering kind' (*Nostromo*, p. 67), the narrator notes in a
specific disclaimer of masculinity in the mentality of Mrs
Gould. But that capacity for the tender action belongs to her
as well as to the 'stout, loud-voiced lady of French extraction'
who reluctantly turned down the appeal of the elder Gould
when he first attempted to refuse the government of Costaguana's assignment to him of the derelict silver mine. 'That
florid person, when approached on behalf of Mr Gould in a
proper manner, and with a suitable present, shook her head
despondently. She was good-natured, and her despondency
was genuine. She imagined she could not take money in
consideration of something she could not accomplish'
(op. cit., p. 55). That honesty and the rueful expression of
the awareness of limits upon personal will illustrate the
feminine in the political world. It is precisely the combina-

tion of self-scrutiny and the recognition of constraint which characterise the mature Conradian protagonist, and almost without exception that protagonist is female. The capacity for self-scrutiny, allied to the recognition of constraint, depends in turn upon another characteristic rarely found in men: the capacity for empathy, or the intuitive perception of the reality of another. At its most dramatic, the failure of empathy results in the impulsive pistol shot with which Sotillo kills his desperate captive, Hirsch; more subtly, the failure of empathy testifies to the incompleteness of even the familial relationships between men. About Charles Gould, responding to the experience of his father: 'His personal feelings had not been outraged, and it is difficult to resent with proper and durable indignation the physical anguish of another organism, even if that organism is one's own father' (op. cit., p. 59).

The capacity for empathy extends into the public or political realm, for it enables the observant Mrs Gould, 'accompanying her husband all over the province in the search for labour', to see 'the land with a deeper glance than a trueborn Costaguanera could have done' (op. cit., p. 86). With Dr Monygham, driven by torture into a level of self-analysis rare in the men in Conrad's novels, Emilia Gould struggles to distinguish one native baby from another; they share the belief that such identity matters and that it is their common responsibility to ascribe it and to affirm it. The accurate perception of the individual, the proper evaluation of personality, allows Emilia Gould to be the first to notice the likely futility of the 'first civilian president' of Costaguana. Clarity of observation, that is, observation unclouded by failure of self-perception, is by its nature inaccessible to the men of *Nostromo* who act in the political realm without the necessary immersion in the personal. As the narrator notes of Decoud, 'he had pushed the habit of universal raillery to a point where it blinded him to the genuine impulses of his own nature' (op. cit., p. 153). That blindness characterises as well the serene political prophesying of Don Avellanos who 'depended very much upon the devotion of his beloved Antonia. He accepted it in the benighted way of men, who, though made in God's image, are like stone idols without sense before the smoke of certain burnt offerings' (op. cit., p. 140). These succinct statements of character analysis are as incisive as any to be found in *The Secret Agent*, and they testify to the same impatience with politicised men of imperfect self-awareness and virtually no capacity for empathy. Such men are dangerous to themselves and ultimately destructive in the private realm. They may achieve success in the political realm, but often inadvertently, not as a result of judgement but rather through that concatenation of events which Conrad regularly presents as having its own logic not dictated by men.

It is with some contempt that Decoud, apostle of the new state, describes the preoccupations of Emilia Gould:

> As to Mrs Gould, she thinks of her schools, of her hospitals, of the mothers with the young babies, of every sick old man in the three villages. If you were to turn your head now you would see her extracting a report from that sinister doctor in a check shirt – what's his name? Monygham – or else catechizing Don Pepe or perhaps listening to Padre Román. They are all down here today – all her ministers of state (op. cit., p. 189).

Those preoccupations, of course, and those conversations, represent the social foundations of the state which Decoud imagines onto paper. Conrad clearly implies the frivolity of Decoud's intellectual enterprise in the face of Emilia Gould's pragmatic intuition. His eventual decline into a despairing solipsism parallels her descent into a loneliness whose personal devastation does not halt her political effectiveness.

In his letters to his sister, the only woman whose intelligence Decoud trusts, he reveals his assessment of the inner strength and power of the South American women, even as he trivialises their condition: 'the women of our country are worth looking at during a revolution', he writes. 'The rouge and pearl powder fall off, together with that passive attitude towards the outer world which education, tradition, custom impose upon them from earliest infancy' (op. cit., p. 234). What he discerned in his sister's face, again from earliest infancy, was her intelligence, 'instead of that

patient and resigned cast which appears when some com-
motion tears down the wall of cosmetics and usage.' It is
characteristic of Decoud to exempt himself and his sister, a
projection of himself, from the condition of the responsibility
for the conditions which govern the lives of those seemingly
unintelligent women who cope so well with tragedy and
revolution when it is thrust upon them. In these highly
political novels, all behaviour and all consequences are in
some sense political; though Claire Rosenfield is but one
critic who emphasises the mythic qualities of Sulaco, the
political confinement of women is not metaphorical. Nor is
the understanding about politics to which Mrs Gould comes
simply personal or emotionally revealing. In contrast to
Decoud's characterisation of himself and his actions as
finally those of an 'adventurer . . . the descendent of
adventurers', Emilia Gould crystallises a conception of
politics which is neither male nor female but *responsible*
(clearly in keeping with the theorising of Gilligan in regard
to the development of moral philosophy): 'It had come into
her mind that for life to be large and full, it must contain the
care of the past and of the future in every passing moment
of the present. Our daily work must be done to the glory of
the dead, and for the good of those who come after' (op. cit.,
p. 521). Intelligence alone, as Decoud discovers to his ultimate
cost, provides neither sanctuary nor response to the indifference of the universe. Just before his suicide, Decoud 'beheld
the universe as a succession of incomprehensible images'
(op. cit., p. 498). It is important to realise that this recognition, so shattering to Decoud, is the bedrock of Conrad's
own thought, expressed in letters and texts throughout his
life; further, it is not withheld from important women characters who know these things and are still determined upon
what Emilia Gould characterises as 'the care of the past and
of the future'.

That loneliness should be at the heart of the human
condition comes as no surprise to Conrad's women. A
generation of critics has seen Emilia Gould in *Nostromo* and
Natalia Haldin in *Under Western Eyes* as touching, even
heart-wrenching women. What they have denied to such
women has been their deserved stature as political actors

in a political world which must make its own meaning. Conrad's distaste for programmatic politics was clear throughout his life. In personal letters, essays (such as 'Autocracy and War'), and in novels as apolitical as *The Nigger of the 'Narcissus'* or as explicitly political as *Under Western Eyes*, Conrad pillories characters who spout political jargon. Most particularly, Conrad exposes the discrepancy between the jargon of compassion and personal behaviour which illuminates the selfishness and self-delusion of the individual. Donkin, in *The Nigger of the 'Narcissus'* and Peter Ivanovitch in *Under Western Eyes* are but two of the glaring examples of such *poseurs*. Not political action but self-deluded theoretical pronouncements serve as the source of Conrad's irony and condemnation. Since from the earliest works women illustrate self-knowledge, along with a sharp focus on the particular and the immediate, women necessarily emerge as more integrated political actors than do men. The integration, especially, between the private and the public realms is consistently available to women. The application of theory to the life of the individual is always evident to women. *Nostromo* is the first novel to elevate that understanding to a full-scale political credo. The cost of capitalism as the commodification of individual life is expressed not through the language of political theory but through the experience of Emilia Gould and her persistent refusal to express such commodification herself.

The political sophistication of a commitment to continuity is not readily apparent to every man of public importance in Sulaco, nor has it been apparent to every critic of *Nostromo*. Within the novel, those who sustain the values of the state, in the form of schools, hospitals, familial relationships, are regarded tenderly but without intellectual admiration. Antonia's political intelligence inspires amazement in Martin Decoud: 'he was ready to believe that some startlingly profound remark, some appreciation of character, or a judgment upon an event, bordered on the miraculous' (op. cit., p. 83). The narrative tone here surely suggests that this condescension reveals volumes about Decoud's own limited appreciation of the capacities of women. A recent woman critic, however, comments that 'this low opinion of women's intelligence is no doubt Conrad's as well as Decoud's' with no other evidence.[6] Emilia Gould, like Antonia Avellanos, finds expression and evaluation through her own thoughts, through the remarks of the omniscient narrator, and through the assumptions and perceptions of a number of male characters. Most often it is Dr Monygham who thinks of her and projects her in his imagination; not surprisingly, Mrs Gould's fragility and vulnerability speak to Dr Monygham and, through him, to the reader. It is the claim she makes upon his imagination 'exalted by a spiritual detachment from the usual sanctions of hope and reward' which impels Dr Monygham into impetuous and dangerous behaviour, 'extremely dangerous to himself and to others, all his scruples vanishing in the proud feeling that his devotion was the only thing that stood between an admirable woman and a frightful disaster' (op. cit., p. 431). This somewhat patronising devotion necessarily rests on the doctor's sense of Emilia Gould's own strength to defend herself in the complex world of Sulaco. While the men who love and admire her see Mrs Gould in this extraordinarily tender fashion, the narrator notes: 'she bore a whole two months of wandering very well; she had that power of resistance to fatigue which one discovers here and there in some quite frail-looking women with surprise – like a state of possession by a remarkably stubborn spirit' (op. cit., pp. 88–9).

In short, there are a number of indications in the narrative method of *Nostromo* that the power and the authenticity of women as political agents is more considerable than the male characters or commentators can credit or describe. Critics continue to deny this, for example Helen Funk Rieselbach, who confuses Decoud's assessment of Antonia with Conrad's. It is part of the unthinking determination of gender-based identity which causes or allows male characters to devalue, ignore, or patronise the particular strengths, intelligence, and endurance of the women. Regular analytical comments from the omniscient narrator suggest that the author constructs some distance between the characters' perceptions of the women and his own. This is not surprising, for Emilia Gould, Antonia Avellanos, and 'the lady of French extraction' follow the successful creation of earlier women who present powerful political and moral commentaries upon the social and political behaviour of the male progatonists. What distinguishes these mature novels is not solely the power of the characterisations, or the subtle indictment of patriarchal and imperialist politics and economic systems, but the rather more direct identification of the women characters as the political agents themselves – the 'subjects' of the texts.

The identification of women as the moral and political agents of these novels seems relatively forthright; it was Conrad, after all, who identified Winnie Verloc as the heroine of *The Secret Agent*: '*this* book is *that* story', as he noted. But to identify Winnie Verloc (or Emilia Gould) as the heroine is not simply to argue for one character (female) over another character (male). Rather, recognition of the central argument of these novels as resting within the behaviour and values of women characters is to restate the arguments substantially. The characters and conditions of the women in these texts constitute a complex criticism and alternative to the cultural values lived out by the male characters whom Conrad treats with such regular irony. It seems clear in *Nostromo* that a perceptible difference in tone characterises the descriptions of some male and some female characters.

This discrepancy is a great deal more marked in *The Secret Agent*, and it is a good deal more significant. This novel is almost universally described as savagely ironic. There is virtually no critical departure from the received wisdom which declares that 'the world of *The Secret Agent* is a world almost totally without morality, where ethical standards and personal loyalties are absent.'[7] Another critical remark, entirely consistent with the critical history of *The Secret Agent*, asserts that 'it is a stroke of wicked humor that the only charitable character in the novel is an idiot', who is also the 'one person whose fate authenticates the disgust Conrad feels for his contemporary society.'[8] Assumptions about Conrad's inability to create credible female protagonists contribute to the difficulty of clearing away from *The Secret Agent* the web of misconceptions that entangle it. Feminist literary critics are among those who contribute to the difficulty: Carolyn Heilbrun remarked in 1973 that 'Conrad could no more have conceived of a woman hero than could Dickens.'[9] Unsurprisingly, *The Secret Agent* resembles the work of Dickens, especially the work which focuses on the madness and depravity of the heartless life of London – *Bleak House* (which actually contains not one but two women heroes). Jocelyn Baines, in his lengthy summing-up of *The Secret Agent*, asserts that probably 'Conrad intended her [Winnie Verloc] to be a sort of feminine counterpart of MacWhirr [the hero of 'Typhoon'], but she does not emerge as a very sympathetic or admirable character.'[10]

Though her plight might evoke sympathy, Baines believes that Winnie Verloc arouses neither pity nor concern in the reader until the very end, when she is betrayed by Comrade Ossipon. Baines' justification for his assertions about Winnie's inability to compel sympathy from the reader (assumed, as always, to be a male reader) tells a good deal about the central difficulty presented by this text for any but the most receptive audience. The bargain struck with life by Winnie Verloc and her mother, a bargain familiar in its outlines to almost any female reader, strikes Baines and numerous other critics as either ferociously unkind to Mr Verloc or as beneath serious notice. Baines disparages and diminishes Winnie's sacrifice of love and sexual and emotional fulfilment, her decision to give up the butcher-boy and their hopes for marriage, by deprecating Winnie's sexual capacity. 'Winnie herself is on such a low mental level that one wonders whether there was even an element of choice, therefore of virtue, in her self-sacrifice or whether it was merely as instinctive as an animal's defense of its offspring.'[11] Baines' confident tone here allows for astonishing rhetoric which succeeds casually in reducing the meaning of a woman's life to the instinctual behaviour of the non-human; gender pronouns disappear, as the human sister metamorphoses into the beast and its offspring. Mother love, often exalted so that it becomes a woman's destiny, here melts down into animality: 'there is no tragedy because there is no sense of waste, no suggestion that the characters were made for better things. ... The final effect is of negation and squalor.'[12]

Such a critical analysis, representative of a multitude of responses to this text, depends, of course, on an unexpressed theory of value which allows a genre called 'tragedy' to assume the highest point in a literary hierarchy. Similarly, the association of enraged motherhood with mindless animality depends on that patriarchal fusion of woman and nature which played such a large part in misconceptions of Conrad's earlier work. Squalor, which is inherent in discussions of domestic life, is by its nature ruled out as a 'serious' subject; the natural world, that is the world 'below' and subordinate to the human world, does not produce subject matter suitable for the highest reaches of literature. One does not write tragedy about dogs.

Curiously, the irony of *The Secret Agent* does not figure in critical discussion as a means of controlling and conveying simple rage, though Conrad makes it clear in his Author's Note that the choice of irony as a mode of expression made it possible for him to write at all, given the intensity of the imaginative vision which possessed him and the combination of 'scorn and pity' which demanded expression. Regularly in Conrad's novels and tales the narrative gives expression to outrage evoked by the disparity between the profession of values and the failure or incapacity to embody them in the gritty details of life itself. Jim, Kurtz, Lingard, and a host of other important male protagonists illustrate the disintegration of civilised (male, romantic) behaviour in the face of the demands of the world: nature, barbarity, the East, women. In these mature novels, however, the issues are presented with a clarity and a precision of tone which seems to evoke from critics a determined refusal to acknowledge the new terms. Powerful women emerge in the eyes of their protectors or wooers as fragile, irrational, intuitive, needy, or so corrupted by altruism that they lose humanity entirely. Not Conrad but his limited male characters as he wrote them, not Conrad but his critics, diminish the women in this way. The texts themselves supply ample evidence of the powerful individuality of the women characters and of Conrad's determination to test the nature of the value structure

which assumes the separation of the public and the domestic
realms as well as the natural superiority of the literary and
political value of the public over the private.

An implicit assertion of these three central novels,
concerned as they are with political doctrines, is the
centrality of the domestic world to the construction of the
world of ideas and political action. Simultaneously, the
novels suggest both individually and collectively that
private madness leads to public insanity; public doctrines,
meanwhile, reveal their inhumanity or falsity as they work
on the fabric of domestic relationships. The violent husband
and father who terrorised the childhood of Winnie and
Stevie testifies to a brutal society which experienced a level
of domestic abuse both known and tolerated as a regular
feature of British life. The failure of their mother to protect
them from the 'irascible licensed victualler' forced Winnie
and Stevie into one another's arms. The head of the family,
licensed to provide for them as well as to them, provided a
climate of terror and mutual dependency. Winnie Verloc's
often-quoted assertion that 'life doesn't bear much looking
into' is thus not a simple-minded refusal to think but a
considered response to a life already lived at the hands of a
violent patriarch. Simultaneous self-abnegation, in the sense
of suppressing her own emotional needs, and assertive-
ness, in the sense of putting herself in the line of fire,
characterise Winnie from her earliest childhood. Altruism
on behalf of the more helpless, on the part of the almost
helpless, has been her chosen style for decades. In her way,
Winnie is the true anarchist, for she has learned to have no
faith in systems of social organisation, all of which have
ignored her or let her down. The isolation of the violent
family has been a well-known social phenomenon for cen-
turies. With the death of the violent father, the diminished
family sustained itself on the industry of its women: Winnie
and her mother.

In this book famous for its ironic tone, there is a
noticeable absence of irony in those passages which focus on
the early life of Winnie or on the self-sacrifice of Winnie's
mother. As Winnie, about to part with her mother, remembers
her life, she feels 'an acute pang of loneliness. She had never

been parted from her mother before. They had stood by each other. She felt that they had, and she said to herself that now mother was gone – gone for good. Mrs Verloc had no illusions' (*The Secret Agent*, p. 178). A survivor of a battered childhood, Winnie comprehends her mother's struggle and identifies with her. No denier of her own experience, Winnie feels her approaching loneliness to the full. Conrad's tone, in this and in succeeding pages about Winnie and Stevie's childhood is direct and full of felt anguish.

> She remembered brushing the boy's hair and tying his pinafores – herself in a pinafore still; the consolations administered to a small and badly scared creature by another creature nearly as small but not quite so badly scared; she had the vision of the blows intercepted (often with her own head), of a door held desperately shut against a man's rage (not for very long); of a poker flung once (not very far), which stilled that particular storm into the dumb and awful silence which follows a thunderclap. (op. cit., p. 242)

In this prose, and in that which describes the departure of Winnie's mother to the home for the aged, Conrad achieves a transparent cadence of hurt and pathos. Irony would be a relief, we realise, but the author denies himself the use of irony precisely where it would allow readers to distance themselves from the great sources of pain in this book. The pain of the battered childhood in the familial stronghold of patriarchal relations is central to the purposes of this book.

Those who have written in defence of *The Secret Agent* as a major text in the Conradian canon have defended it for reasons far removed from the character and the centrality of Winnie Verloc and her devotion to her mother and brother. Only when we read this text, in concert with those which precede and follow it, as part of Conrad's long analysis of the centrality of domestic relationships to the success or failure of political and moral systems, do we read it properly. Then the unique capacity of the individual woman, the domestic act, to express the ethical meaning of the novel leaps from its pages. It is in that sense that an early detail of *The Secret Agent* returns to haunt the reader with its multiplicity of meanings: the bottle of marking ink of the opening chapter contains such import when properly understood.

Very early in *The Secret Agent*, the narrator describes the shabby shop owned and presided over by Mr Verloc. Sometimes, he notes, 'it was Mrs. Verloc who would appear at the call of the cracked bell.' Embarrassed to do business with a woman, the male customer 'with rage in his heart would proffer a request for a bottle of marking ink, retail value sixpence (price in Verloc's shop one-and-sixpence), which, once outside, he would drop stealthily into the gutter' (op. cit., p. 5). That unwanted marking ink, associated with the intrusive presence of a woman in the sleazy world of dirty pictures, is the medium through which Winnie attempts to ensure Stevie's safe return home; it is what she uses to write his address in his overcoat, on the scrap of fabric that survives the explosion to bring home to her instead the news of Stevie's destruction and the dissolution of the fantastic conception of safety to which she had sacrificed her happiness. The image of the irritated and disappointed man throwing away the marking ink leads inexorably to the discarded scrap of humanity whose address, alone, does not explode into nothingness. This tight construction, sustained relentlessly to the final refrain, 'An impenetrable mystery', 'will hang forever over this act', 'this act of madness or despair', illustrates for the reader the author's determination to make the entire book indivisible, unified, and as its title page claims, ultimately simple. The redemptive values of *The Secret Agent*, made visible through the clarity of the language and the vision, are the values which Winnie Verloc, her mother, and the lady patroness of the anarchist Michaelis exemplify. The pain inherent in the text seems to have been so potent that perhaps it accounts, at least in part, for the history of critical misconception which has followed the novel since its first reception. The story is about Winnie Verloc; her battered childhood is the source of her devotion, and the heroism exemplified by Winnie and her mother do illuminate the darkness of a life that does not bear much looking into.

That unacknowledged determination *not* to apprehend, *not* to understand, is the most salient characteristic of the narrator of *Under Western Eyes*, the last of the explicitly political novels of the central group of Conrad's maturity. 'Ignorance of her modes of feeling', as the narrator describes his condition at one juncture, characterises the narrative frame. In one sense, of course, the limitations of the teacher of languages specifically apply to his Western political and emotional upbringing; they unfit him for any intuitive comprehension of the Russian temperament. But they unfit him as well, he often reminds the reader, for the power and the subtlety of women's thought and behaviour. For the most part, he confesses to uneasiness in the face of 'deep feeling.' Having brought to Natalia Haldin the news of her brother's execution, he notes that he 'was grateful to Miss Haldin for not embarrassing me by an outward display of deep feeling. I admired her for that wonderful control over herself, even while I was a little frightened of it. It was the stillness of great tension. What if it should suddenly snap?' (*Under Western Eyes*, p. 112). It seems clear that the determination not to understand is in this text explicitly linked to the Western male's fear of great emotion. The splitting of emotion and intellect, characteristic of male behaviour in Conrad's novels as well as in Western thought, creates an incapacity in the narrator to enter the experience of women who are so critical to the moral and political centre of *Under Western Eyes*.

Conrad goes to great lengths in this book to acknowledge, delimit, and transcend the gender-based limitations on character and philosophy that have provided the sources of so much tension in his work from the start. Beginning with Natalia Haldin, he explicitly confronts the conventional definitions and assumptions about female beauty, knowledge, and political activity. The narrator, somewhat embarrassed, reports the effect of Miss Haldin's particular physical presence: 'She directed upon me her grey eyes shaded by black eyelashes, and I became aware, not withstanding my years, how attractive physically her personality could be to a man capable of appreciating in a woman something else than the mere grace of femininity.' With some hesitation, he goes on to describe what a feminist reader might recognise as the androgynous appeal of the young woman, 'whose glance was as direct and trustful as that of a young man', intrepid but not 'aggressive' (op. cit., p. 102). The most salient characteristic of the key Russian characters, particularly Miss Haldin, is their directness; and it is precisely that directness which proves so unsettling and so incomprehensible to the narrator and to other Westerners who encounter them. The narrator regularly takes refuge in his 'Western incomprehension.' He describes himself as 'reduced to silence by [his] ignorance of her modes of feeling. Difference of nationality is a terrible obstacle for our complex Western natures' (op. cit., p. 116). His regular retreat into the safety of 'complexity' is in fact clearly false. Like the critic who denigrated Winnie Verloc in order to disparage her self-sacrifice, the narrator of *Under Western Eyes* ascribes to her a face-saving simplicity of emotional apprehension: 'Miss Haldin probably was too simple to suspect my embarrassment' (op. cit., p. 117). The inability to feel deeply and the reluctance to express feeling, both male characteristics, are thus claimed as complex Western forms of social behaviour. Since the apologetic, intrusive, and ultimately boring nature of the narrator, the professor of languages, tends inevitably to colour his insights, the reader counters his evaluations with another. The impact of Natalia Haldin's sensibility grows as the narrator clearly becomes both more infatuated and less capable of understanding or properly valuing the source of his infatuation.

Since *Under Western Eyes* is one of the few novels in which Conrad focuses directly upon the phenomenon of 'feminism', the novel allows the reader to come to some understanding of what kind of feminist analysis illuminates human experience, as well as the ways in which feminism itself can be perverted and misused. Categorically, *Under Western Eyes* states that a passionate and manipulative 'feminism' which exalts a false idea of womanhood is as unattractive and inherently dangerous as the self-deluded romanticism of the professor of languages. Above all other texts, *Under Western Eyes* seems most focused on the discrepancy between the professed and the real, the abstract and the particular, the universal and the partial. Since feminism has served so well in Western thought as a means of demystifying and dethroning the assertions of universality and objectivity, it is actually an appropriate tool for the analysis of Conrad's method in *Under Western Eyes*. The Russian Peter Ivanovitch, the 'great feminist', has erected feminism into a universalist creed of perfect abstraction. Himself a womaniser and a cruelly offensive taskmaster, oblivious to the individuality of his own women employees and associates, he does not so much invalidate feminism as illustrate the need for a true form of it. As Maureen Fries argues, Peter Ivanovitch is clearly not a true feminist; rather, it is Conrad, having created women who are the 'industrial, mental, political, social and sexual equals of men' who is the real feminist. 'In *Under Western Eyes*', she notes, 'androgyny seems to pose no threat either to Conrad or to his sympathetic male characters.'[13] Recent criticism of *Under Western Eyes* continues to struggle with the unreliable narrator: 'the narrator's bias toward conventional feminine action is of dubious reliability at best. His own version of woman's sentiments makes him simultaneously a source for and a mocker of the values around which the novel ambiguously hovers.'[14] Discounting the narrator, perceiving the women characters in the light of the developing emphasis Conrad places on their complex intelligence and integration of thought and emotion, resolves the ambiguity that the recent critic describes.

The contrast posed between professed belief and actual behaviour always serves to identify the ethical and moral core of Conradian protagonists. The test of the particular, especially in the face of the claims of the abstract, allows the reader to discern the real nature of protagonists often deluded about themselves. *Under Western Eyes* is no exception to this pattern. The abject condition of Tekla immediately destroys the credibility of Peter Ivanovitch not just as a feminist but as a decent person. The subtleties of his abuse, the ways in which viciousness masquerades as tenderness, are immediately clear to Natalia Haldin as they are clear to the reader, despite the fears of the narrator that she will succumb to the lure of the great feminist. That identification of vision between the reader and the heroine is but one of the ways in which Conrad locates the reader securely and eliminates what critics describe as the ambiguity of this novel. Consistent assumptions about masculine points of view have always contributed to critical difficulties with the stature and accomplishments of the women characters in Conrad. Natalia Haldin is only the most immediate example of this process at work.

The vital role of the mature woman in this text is communicated in part through Razumov's awareness of his own emotional fragility because he had no mother. His utter lack of family, but most particularly the deprivation of mothering, has left him a precariously balanced and divided person. Though there may be sympathetic male characters in *Under Western Eyes*, as some critics suggest, there are no mature, unified, integrated men. The narrative consistently reveals the fragmentary nature of male personality. By contrast, the woman revolutionary Sophia Antonovna, illustrates a degree of maturity and personal integration which is compelling. Razumov, quite correctly, fears every conversation with her, because she retains her intuitive awareness of human personality at the same time that she expresses theoretical political arguments. 'How un-Russian she looked, thought Razumov.' It is her incorporation of contrasting yet harmonious qualities which marks the woman revolutionary.

> Razumov looked at her white hair: and this mask of so many uneasy years seemed nothing but a testimony to the invincible vigour of revolt. It threw out into an astonishing relief the unwrinkled face, the brilliant black glance, the upright compact figure, the simple, brisk self-possession of the mature personality – as though, in her revolutionary pilgrimage she had discovered the secret, not of everlasting youth, but of everlasting endurance. (*Under Western Eyes*, pp. 263–4)

Unsurprisingly, it is Sophia Antonovna who pursues the question of Razumov's identity after others are satisfied. She is tenacious, determined to trace the most difficult and demanding enquiries to their ultimate sources. She knows and acknowledges the cost of revolution, and faces the import of Peter Ivanovitch's character as the price of his importance to the eventual transformation of Russia. And it is finally this articulated acknowledgement of the cost of revolution which seems to distinguish the unique political consciousness of some Conradian women. Certainly, such knowledge is represented by Emilia Gould as well as by Sophia Antonovna. The common source for their mature incorporation of different ways of knowing may well have been Conrad's mother, Ewa Korzeniowska.

Strength in a woman may take many forms: it is apparent in Conrad's novels that the appearance of physical delicacy may conceal great stamina, strength of will, and mental toughness. Emilia Gould, with her masses of fair hair balanced on a delicate head, testifies to the inner resiliency of a slight figure. There is as well a moral and intellectual strength, characteristic of what we know of Ewa Korzeniowska, which remarkably resembles the physical slightness of Emilia Gould coupled with characteristics of Natalia Haldin: the open-eyed contemplation of desperate alternatives and widespread suffering. In her written accounts of prison visits to Apollo in 1861, Ewa testifies to the willed tranquillity of spirit which holds in balance great emotions, precisely the serenity so precariously displayed by Natalia Haldin at the conclusion of *Under Western Eyes*.

Ewa describes the strict regulations concerning prison visits which allowed her to see her husband for a maximum of one five-minute visit per month. 'Only once', she writes, 'on Christmas Eve, we [wives and mothers] were allowed to clasp the prisoners' hands and break wafers with them; but the regular visits are different; a closely woven wire mesh separates visitors from prisoners; words freeze on the lips amidst repeated cries of "not allowed" by numerous witnesses.' The close observation, the meticulous description, prepare the reader for Ewa's final summary of the prison experience:

> I had a problem: he had been ill, poor darling, but now he is almost well again. The lack of exercise and the [erratic] heat of prison must have affected his health. But he is in good spirits, calm and relaxed and during our short and rare meetings we can really joke about things. This is permitted. The sight of tears is not liked and I must say they are never seen.[15]

The temptation of the observer, like that of the Western

professor of languages, is to attribute to such sustained emotional restraint a triumph over the self, indeed, the disappearance of the self. It is with a sense of exile that the professor, at the end of *Under Western Eyes*, testifies to the impression that Natalia Haldin is disappearing even as he observes her. As he describes her new dimension of serenity, it is the result of her having ceased 'to think of herself.' To the professor, her loss is evidence of her Russian soul triumphing over her very selfhood. But there are other, better, explanations to which the letters and recollections of Ewa and Apollo Korzeniowski contribute.

The inability of the Western professor of languages, and the other male intellectuals and political activists in this group of Conrad novels, to lose or find themselves fully in action testifies not to their maturity or political sophistication but to their fear of dissolving, as indeed Martin Decoud does dissolve, without the reassurance of human, usually female, companionship and support. The inner strength and integration of personality necessary to allow a complex and complete devotion to an act, a cause, or a political course of action lies beyond the capacities of the male protagonists of these novels. It does not, however, lie outside the abilities of the women who remind us, in their sometimes lonely maturity, of Ewa Korzeniowska. Like Natalia Haldin, Ewa looked to eventual concord with a realistic awareness of the intervening years of struggle and loss. ' "I must own to you" ', Natalia Haldin says near the end of *Under Western Eyes*,

'that I shall never give up looking forward to the day when all discord shall be silenced. Try to imagine its dawn! The tempest of blows and of execrations is over; all is still; the new sun is rising, and the weary men, united at last, taking count in their conscience of the ended contest, feel saddened by their victory, because so many ideas have perished for the triumph of one, so many beliefs have abandoned them without support. They feel alone on the earth and gather close together.' (op. cit., pp. 376–7)

The tone of Natalia Haldin's last remarks, at once resolute and lucid, may remind one of the tone of Ewa Korzeniowska's letters. 'The sight of tears is not liked and I must say they

are never seen.' There is an awareness of cost, an acknowledgement of terrible loss, and a quiet assertion of emotional
self-control. Unlike the male protagonists, from Verloc to
Razumov, these women have no fear of emotion or of their
ability to contain it. The women of these novels, like Ewa
Korzeniowska, experience great loneliness; unlike the men,
they also share with Emilia Gould the sustaining sense of
connection to the past and to the future. Bearing in his
memory a relationship between his parents of great emotional
warmth and political commitment, Conrad surely knew
both the rewards and the perils of such experience. Its traces
are evident throughout the great novels of his maturity, but
nowhere more evidently than in the creation and development of Natalia Haldin in *Under Western Eyes*.

CHAPTER FIVE

Identification

With his last novels, Conrad began to explore a particularly difficult and problematical aspect of women's lives: the connections and the conflicts between women. In a series of novels better known for their focus on romantic love, Conrad considered the ways in which women, through heterosexual relationships themselves, were often separated from significant women figures whom they needed for purposes of identification, growth, and security. At the same time, then, that the theme of romantic love became significant, in novels that in the opinion of many critics suffer from this focus, the theme of women's needs for one another came to be a dramatic sub-text in the novels with which Conrad's career and life came to an end.

Chance, published in 1913, provided the financial and popular success that had eluded Conrad earlier in his writing career. It was ostensibly 'romantic' in its plot, focusing on the shy and diffident Captain Anthony's protection and love for Flora De Barral, and culminating in a marriage which emphasised tortured restraint and chivalry until its dramatic consummation. The novel presents a number of problematical issues for modern readers, particularly the nature of Marlow's consistently misogynistic tone which colours the narration. Feminist readers of the early novels and tales for which Marlow serves as narrator have some grounding in the meaning and effect of his attitudes towards women. With *Chance*, Conrad regularly juxtaposes events of emotional and personal tenderness to a narrative tone of brutality and sarcasm, extremes not present in his earlier use of Marlow. The novel seems in its very structure to exemplify the struggle of women to make their voices heard over, under and around a male discourse determined to give its own shape and meaning to the lives of women subjects. Even critics who recognise the verdicts on women and feminism as Marlow's rather than Conrad's may not adequately address the effect of the narrative method on the struggle of the ostensible heroine; such critics include both Rieselbach and Brodie, both concerned with Conrad's feminism.

Like *Lord Jim*, *Chance* emerges for the reader in a complex series of narrative and time shifts. If we understand the central theme of the book to involve the desperate difficulty of a woman attempting to live and tell her own story, the narrative obscurities exemplify the life experience of Flora De Barral, the Damsel of the text. Rieselbach notes that, like *Under Western Eyes*, *Chance* has a heroine 'who at first appear[s a] predestined victim but later prove[s] strong.'[1] There is an air of collusion in *Chance*, a strange atmosphere in which a variety of men seem to conspire to aid Flora while in reality they seek to muffle her voice, to negate her individuality, all in the guise of kindness and altruistic concern. That strange collusiveness begins with the Author's Note, in which Conrad adopts a more than usually defensive tone. He writes: 'I can not sufficiently insist upon the truth that when I sit down to write my intentions are always blameless however deplorable the ultimate effect of the art may turn out to be' (p. x).

With the exception of the desperate financier, De Barral, the men in *Chance* are all noteworthy for their 'blamelessness'. Each is portrayed, or portrays himself, as wholly devoted to the welfare of Flora, while among them they virtually torture her with reminders of her neediness, her dependency and her fragility. In reality, Flora is a cheerful, hardy, poised and self-reliant young woman filled with a desire to love and to be loved, to experience her own sexuality and capacity for romance. Her father wishes to keep her a child, and those around her attempt to deny the very qualities that define her as a woman and an adult.

Marlow, most of all, expresses a hostility to Flora's person which testifies to his raging distaste for her in any guise except abject helplessness. Encountering Flora at the edge of the quarry as she contemplates suicide, Marlow snarls with an irritability that suggests an investment on his part in her passivity rather than in her attempts to solve the problem of her life. 'I was nettled by her brusque manner of asserting her folly', he comments, 'and I told her that neither did I [care] as far as that went, in a tone that almost suggested that she was welcome to break her neck for all I cared. This was considerably more than I meant, but I don't like rude girls' (*Chance*, p. 45).

Flora's 'rudeness' consists of her straightforward account of her sadness and feeling of abandonment; Marlow prefers her in the guise of passivity, as he confesses a moment later. 'She looked unhappy. And I don't know how to say it – well – it suited her. The clouded brow, the pained mouth, the vague fixed glance! A victim. And this characteristic aspect made her attractive; an individual touch – you know' (op. cit., pp. 45–6). The voice of Marlow, impatient, rude, sarcastic, has not been adequately examined by critics who attribute to his presence complexity but not the sheer malevolence that the narrator himself admits. A typical analysis in 1982 by the critic Daniel Schwartz suggests simply that:

> *Chance* has historical interest as an unintentional parody of the self-conscious narrator that was perfected by James, Ford and Conrad. Like most parodies, *Chance* teaches us something about the limitations and possibilities of the form that is caricatured.'[2]

Speculations about the mode of narration that disregard the particular virulence of Marlow's language suggest that it is of no consequence when, in fact, the hostility towards women that Marlow unashamedly projects has everything to do with the effect of the novel on its readers. Schwartz notes that 'the reader becomes anaesthetised to the characters' passions and to dramatic situations because they are remote from his experience.'[3] However, another response to the complex levels of narration might be an impatient determination to get to the centre of the circular structure, a sense of frustrated identification with Flora who disappears at the will of Marlow and returns only when he is ready to allow her. Schwartz asserts that the narrative complexity deprives the book of a form which might unify the sensations of the characters and the readers. But if one considers Marlow's distaste as a unifying element in itself, a feminist reader may come to a new appreciation of Flora's struggle within the text for her life and against a narrator determined to frustrate, even dismiss, her attempts to speak for herself. Rieselbach and Brodie wrestle with the antagonism towards feminism which Marlow expresses but seem helpless to explain his venomous tone. Some repudiation of Marlow, which Conradian critics appear unwilling to risk, would provide a relatively straightforward and simple explanation: on some level, *Chance* might represent Conrad's separation from Marlow in a final form.

The determination on the part of critics to fuse Conrad with Marlow, despite Conrad's regular disclaimers of such mixed identity, reach a new pitch with the appearance of Marlow in *Chance*. Since Marlow's *persona* is so clearly unpleasant in this novel, while it was only marginally problematical to non-feminist readers in *Heart of Darkness* and *Lord Jim*, critics of the late novels must work hard to explain away the final characterisation that distinguishes Marlow as the narrator of *Chance*. If he is as sneering as he asserts, it would hardly be comfortable to identify him as Conrad's *alter ego*; yet there are the usual unmistakable similarities between their positions. Like Conrad, Marlow wrestles with his status as a seaman on land, a teller of tales, a man of detachment tempted regularly to involve himself in domestic affairs. Yet his pronouncements are so extreme and self-revealing that the critic must resort to some complex manipulation to save the author from his narrator. 'He is a surrogate for Conrad's middle-age prejudices rather than for his quest for values and for emotional stability.'[4]

For the feminist reader who identified Marlow from his earliest appearances as a *narrative voice* in the control of the author, rather than as the projection of the author, Marlow in *Chance* provides no such problem. His revulsion in the face of the assertive woman, his desire to see Flora as victim forever, fit effortlessly into the development of the character who emerged so clearly in the early works: frightened and suspicious of passionate women, comfortable with himself as one who perpetuated the ignorance and deprivation of women whose lives were defined by the imperialism that tarnished the image of Marlow himself. A final repudiation of Marlow seems a politically consistent action for Conrad to take as he turns his attention more fully to domestic drama.

Within *Chance*, violent domestic relations emerge as the shaping forces which damage personality and make the attainment of secure adulthood a perilous enterprise. Men as well as women, growing up in households dominated by abusive fathers, come to mature ages without having attained maturity itself; they remain passive, anxious, self-doubting. Such households do not emerge for the first time in *Chance*, of course. Conrad wrote at length in *The Secret Agent* of the devastating effect of the violent and abusive father upon a household, and as early as *An Outcast of the Islands* he identified the abuse of a wife as behaviour both recognised and ignored by European society. *Chance*, however, represents a powerful departure from earlier treatments of such abuse and violence, for Marlow's revelation of his own tendency to blame the victim and enjoy her victimisation creates a new atmosphere in Conrad's work. The issue of complicity has been important throughout Conrad's writing; but that complicity until *Chance* has been more conventionally defined within the political and moral realm. With this novel, domestic relations constitute the whole canvas on which the characters are drawn. What many critics regard as the 'uncongenial' subject matter of love and marriage is not different from earlier novels in kind so much as it is radically different in degree. There is no escape, in *Chance*, from the causes and consequences of psychological damage, no respite in political or economic life from the consideration of personal responsibility and psychic loss.

Perhaps it is this claustrophobic focus on domestic drama that accounts for the critical uneasiness with *Chance*.

Earlier novels were not without romantic or domestic relationships, but those were not the sole subjects of the narration. In the group of novels which represents the final constellation of works, Conrad chose to put relationships at their centres, without political activity that might, in the eyes of some readers, 'balance' the concerns of the characters. Given the unconcealed hostility of the narrator, Marlow, Flora De Barral's need for a sympathetic friend plays a more important role than a young woman's desire for contact with other women might otherwise. Lacking a mother, Flora turns first to a governess who chooses rather to fend for her own future by abandoning Flora in favour of a liaison with a man who, as Marlow puts it, 'can struggle to get a place for himself or perish.' This remark comes in the course of a lengthy paragraph in which Marlow articulates fully his conception of a woman's place in the world:

> But a woman's part is passive, say what you like, and shuffle the facts of the world as you may, hinting at lack of energy, of wisdom, of courage. As a matter of fact, almost all women have all of that – of their own kind. But they are not made for attack. Wait they must. I am speaking here of women who are really women. And it's no use talking of opportunities, either. I know that some of them do talk of it. But not the genuine women. Those know better. (*Chance*, p. 281)

In this passage, because he is safely confining women to a passivity which is by its nature non-threatening, Marlow adopts a tone of dispassionate ease. Only when he refers to particular women, especially as they reach out to one another, does he resort to the snarling tone of his remarks about Flora's thoughts about suicide.

The novel is rich in examples of women attempting to succour one another but succumbing to the imperatives of social mobility and economic security. It is women's force, what Marlow calls the 'force of nature, blind in its strength and capricious in its power' (op. cit., p. 327) that accounts for Marlow's defensive hostility. Any sign of self-assuredness, of a sense of responsibility or connection between women, evokes from Marlow outbursts of fearful hostility. The individual woman, even the woman under siege, such as

Flora, has a potential for power. Women in relation to one another suggest to Marlow a terrifying capacity for destruction. 'In all of them', he remarks, 'termagant, flirt, crank, washerwoman, blue-stocking, outcast and even in the ordinary fool of the ordinary commerce there is something left, if only a spark. And where there is a spark there can always be a flame . . .' (Conrad's ellipsis, p. 353). For Marlow, Mrs Fyne's attempts to make Flora self-sufficient are the mad blunderings of a lesbian harridan; he despises her feminist credo, as he understands it:

> It was a knock-me-down doctrine – a practical individualistic doctrine. You would not thank me for expounding it to you at large. Indeed I think that she herself did not enlighten me fully. There must have been things not fit for a man to hear. But shortly, and as far as my bewilderment allowed me to grasp its naive atrociousness, it was something like this: That no consideration, no delicacy, no tenderness, no scruples should stand in the way of a woman (who by the mere fact of her sex was the predestined victim of conditions created by men's selfish passions, their vices, and their abominable tyranny) from taking the shortest cut towards securing for herself the easiest possible existence. She had even the right to go out of existence without considering anyone's feelings or convenience, since some women's existences were made impossible by the short-sighted harshness of men. (op. cit., p. 59)

An attentive reader, especially one with some feminist perspective, recognises in this diatribe Marlow's outrage at women's self-determination and the identification of patriarchy *as a system* at the heart of a situation of inequality. Suicide, one form of asserting ownership of her own life, Flora's briefly contemplated act, must be particularly infuriating because, like abortion, it asserts fully a woman's rights over her body, the life it bears. Mrs Fyne's wretched childhood, which illuminated for her the tyranny inherent in patriarchy, Marlow dismisses: 'The Fynes were excellent people, but Mrs Fyne wasn't the daughter of a domestic tyrant for nothing. There were no limits to her revolt' (op. cit., p. 62). The reader who remembers Conrad's narrative tone in *The Secret Agent* when he recounted Winnie Verloc's terror as 'the daughter of a domestic tyrant' cannot confuse Marlow's attitude with Conrad's. Rather, the reader is enabled to chart the collapse of Marlow's defences against the urgency of women's determination to achieve private happiness within a safe environment. Chance, according to Marlow, rules the world and works against the attainment of human happiness; but Flora achieves happiness, often through her display of affection and trust towards women such as the stewardess who cared for her when she was exhausted and hungry. Mrs Fyne's desire for Flora to achieve autonomy without marriage, without dependency on a man, strikes Marlow as unwomanly and outrageous.

Mrs Fyne's outrage at the marriage between her brother, Captain Anthony, and Flora reassures Marlow of women's fundamental inhumanity towards one another. But the variety of feminism chosen by Mrs Fyne, with its fearful contemplation of the institution of marriage, accounts in large part for her disappointment in Flora. Not hatred of women but deep-seated fear of conventional marriage animates Mrs Fyne and evokes her harsh response to Flora's situation. Programmatic feminism which adheres to abstract dicta rather than to individual needs always received short shrift from Conrad; certainly the figure of Peter Ivanovitch in *Under Western Eyes* illustrates the distaste Conrad felt for such self-righteous ideologues. At the same time, however, beneath Marlow's intense dislike for Mrs Fyne lies the clear presentation of the domestic violence from which Mrs Fyne longs to protect Flora and all other young women, a determination Conrad respects quite as much as his narrator despises it.

In the end, the virtue that Marlow allows to Flora is her capacity for endurance, though events in the narrative illustrate more than such a term might indicate. Flora's ability to communicate her youth, her energy, and her 'pluckiness' serves her despite the narrator's determination to constrain her. Frederick R. Karl suggests, drawing attention to the symbolic names of women characters in the later novels, that Conrad sought to present women in triumphant mode towards the end of his career. 'Rather than calling him a misogynist in this period, that is, by transferring

Marlow's statements to him, we find Conrad trying to reflect sympathetically the current conflicts of women, who were then so much in the news as they sought the vote just before the war.'5 For Karl, the layers of narrative that, in effect, stand between Flora and the reader do not relate to her struggle but to Conrad's need to connect with modernism. And in general that is the critical position in regard to *Chance*, a position which makes the voice and the person of Flora and the other women in the text almost incidental, oddly crediting Conrad with good intentions towards women without close consideration of the way in which narrative method itself expresses women's struggles.

But the women in the last series of novels refuse to endure quietly their absence from the centres of critical speculation. Lena, in *Victory*, like Flora who precedes her and Rita who follows her, projects both fragility and determination. As Najder notes, among Conrad's works, '*Victory* remains artistically apart.'6 In it, most explicitly, Conrad distinguishes a woman's determination to connect, to forge a life of relationship with a man's commitment to detachment, distance, and withdrawal. Lena's early account of her situation testifies to her energy and her realism: ' "A girl can always put up a fight. You believe me? Only it isn't easy to stand up for yourself when you feel there's nothing and nobody at your back. There's nothing so lonely in the world as a girl who has got to look after herself" ' (*Victory*, p. 85). There is a straightforwardness to Lena (as Heyst renames her) which is consistent with the straightforward nature of the narrative in *Victory*.

Again, there is in this novel testimony to the need women have of one another, to their sensitivity to one another's different forms of captivity and service. While a male voice identifies Schomberg's wife as 'too unattractive to be anything else' (op. cit., p. 38), Lena comprehends immediately the nature of her situation – and her capacity for sympathy. ' "I tell you she daren't open her mouth to him. And she isn't as silly as she looks. She wouldn't give us away. She knows a trick or two of that. She'll help – that's what she'll do, if she dares to do anything at all" ' (op. cit., p. 88). And of course Mrs Schomberg does help, not once but twice in the course of the novel, both times at terrifying risk. For once again the backdrop to the action of a novel by Conrad consists of a violent and abusive domestic relationship in which a woman exists regularly in a condition of panic and servility. And, as in the earlier depictions of such domestic relations, the onlookers share both casual knowledge and perfect detachment. Hesyt's commitment to detachment, the ostensible centre of the novel, is but an extreme form of the condition displayed by all the men in the text. Davidson, the bluff and good-hearted sailor who cares about Heyst, describes without emphasis the prevailing mode of behaviour, the lack of interest in intervention even into agreed-upon misery. When Heyst remarks that Schomberg ' "seems to be an unconscionable ruffian" ', Davidson replies: ' "We here have got used to him . . . I'd hardly call him that. I only know him as a hotel-keeper' " (op. cit., p. 55).

Heyst's uncharacteristic act of rescuing Lena takes on additional meaning in the face of society's perfect acquiescence in the victimisation of women, whether in the shabby all-girls orchestra or in the visibly brutal domestic relationship played out in public over long years. The consistent backdrop of domestic abuse suggests the difficulty of the romantic fiction to which Conrad turned in these late novels. The protagonists not only must struggle towards one another burdened by their individual personalities and differences but do so in a world characterised by long-standing and tacitly accepted relationships built on male abuse and female servility and fear.

For the important women characters, those background relationships complicate the search for women friends, models and mentors. The heroines of the last novels express their longing for women friends: Flora, in *Chance*, remembers Mrs Fyne as the woman who was so kind to her, quite in spite of Marlow's interpretation. For Marlow, women's loyalty is to 'their common femininity which they behold triumphant with a secret and proud satisfaction' (op. cit., p. 371). But for the young women of the texts the desire for mothers, friends and sisters is rather the desire for a sense of likeness, for a person to trust, for an image to study and consider as an example. The rivalry and jealousy between women, as in the all-women orchestra in *Victory*, is especially hurtful to the young protagonists who, without mothers, suffer acute loneliness at the same time that they form their conception of what it will mean to be a woman. For Lena in *Victory*, as for Flora in *Chance*, growing up motherless has meant a commitment to stand by her father, to take her identity from a relationship with a man without his own woman.

Both *Victory* and *Chance*, then, explore the consequences for women who grow up not only motherless but deprived of the opportunity to develop as women securely connected to other women. Much of the tortured sense of dependence and unworthiness that Flora and Lena experience comes from the sense of being treated kindly by men in a world in which such treatment appears anachronistic. Isolated from women friends, pursued by men who attempt to use them for their own reasons, these heroines sacrifice themselves on behalf of the only men who treat them decently. Mutuality of relationship is hinted at in *Chance*, out of the question in *Victory* until it is too late. The overt consequences of solitary coming of age for a woman are implicit in both books, but not until the character of Rita in *The Arrow of Gold* does a woman speak openly and pointedly of the need for women in a young woman's life.

In her first lengthy appearance in the novel, Rita describes her sudden entry into the adult world, with the death of her protector, Henry Allegre: ' "Listen," ' she says, ' "I don't need to justify myself, but if I had known a single woman in the world, if I had only had the opportunity to observe a single one of them, I would have been perhaps on my guard. But you know I hadn't. The only woman I had anything to do with was myself, and they say that one can't know oneself" ' (*The Arrow of Gold*, p. 84). With Rita de Lastaola, as she calls herself, the implicit search for female models of development becomes, finally, overt.

The lost mother, so often a feature of the male protagonist's experience, now finally becomes the distinguishing mark of the woman at the heart of the novel. ' "I never knew my mother" ', Rita tells the narrator. ' "I don't even know how she looked. There are no paintings or photographs in our farmhouse amongst the hills. I haven't even heard her described to me. I believe I was never good enough to be told these things" ' (op. cit., p. 113). There is, of course, great pathos in these revelations, which contribute to the impression of a lonely young woman. Unlike the earlier heroines, however, Rita possesses both power and a degree of self-confidence. Her analysis of her limitations, focused as it is on her inability to learn how to be a woman from other women, is especially cogent because she has the resources of wealth and status which Conrad denied to his earlier heroines in these last novels. Rita's rural childhood, her detachment from the conventional world, provide for her the sort of marginality which allows her to comment on her situation with some candour. Craving sisterhood, she has a real sister who detests her godlessness, her directness, her involvement in the world of politics and power. For all her sexual magnetism, she inspires an immediate liking and affection in the narrator because of her youthful energy. He imagines her at sea with him on a gun-running expedition, an androgynous sailor:

> But what a charming, gentle, gay, and fearless companion she would have made! I believed in her fearlessness in any adventure that would interest her. It would be a new occasion for me, a new viewpoint for that faculty of admiration she had awakened in me at sight – at first sight – before she opened her lips – before she ever turned her eyes on me. She would have to wear some sort of sailor costume, a blue woollen shirt open at the throat . . . Dominick's hooded cloak would envelop her amply, and her face under the black hood would have a luminous quality, adolescent charm and an enigmatic expression (Conrad's ellipsis) (*The Arrow of Gold*, p. 149)

In some sense, the narrator, Monsieur George as he is called, attempts to redefine Rita's femininity, her identity as a woman. He emphasises their shared youth, their affinity for one another's personalities, while all the while Rita longs for identification with other women. Explicitly, the narrator (who may well be based on Conrad during his own complicated gun-running days) denies any affinity between Rita and her sister. His musings suggest that Rita's individuality rests on her separation from a world of women, testing the notion that there is no deep connection among women that might survive the apparent differences.

> Contrary to what generally happens, it was when one saw those two women together that one lost all belief in the possibility of their relationship near or far. It extended even to their common humanity. One, as it were, doubted it. If one of the two was representative, then the other was something more or less than human. One wondered whether these two women belonged to the same scheme of creation. One was secretly amazed to see them standing together, speaking to each other, having words in common, understanding each other. (op. cit., pp. 121–2)

In this important paragraph, the narrator suggests an extravagant image from which he distances himself with the regular use of the pronoun 'one.' It is his wish that Rita should exist in perfect isolation (loneliness, as she experiences it) from which only he may rescue her by virtue of their affinity which, though charged with sexual tension, the narrator imagines to be beyond sexuality or gender.

In some ways, this tender approach to Rita de Lastaola contains more danger to a woman than even Marlow's overt hostility and sarcasm. For Marlow, clearly, envisions women as powerful both individually and collectively. He recognises the connections between and among women and, fearing those connections, does what he can to play upon the fears and confusions of women in order to keep them apart. But Monsieur George, despite his transparent love for Rita and his apparent good will towards her, secretly damages her more powerfully than Marlow could ever damage Flora, in his serene appropriation of her female humanity. And George persists in this vision of Rita despite the attempts at intervention by other women in the text.

A number of women characters in *The Arrow of Gold* speak about Rita, all of them recognising capacities in her which they experience in themselves. Despite Monsieur George's need to disconnect Rita from the world of women, they respond to her immediately and feelingly. Madame Leonore, the wife of the master seaman Dominic, speaks directly of her natural connection to Rita. ' "You see" ', she

says, ' "we women are not like you men, indifferent to each
other unless by some exception. Men say we are always
against one another, but that's only men's conceit." ' A
moment later, continuing to muse upon Rita, she notes that
she, like Rita, had a face of her own, ' "though not so superb.
And I, too, didn't know why I had come into the world any
more than she does" ' (op. cit., p. 134). Dominic, in response
to her last words, suggests to his wife that now she knows
why she has come into the world: it is clear that he intends
her to acknowledge their long partnership, but she resists
his demand and returns to her concern for Rita. Strongly,
she asserts ' "She is for no man! She would be vanishing
out of their hands like water that cannot be held." ' The
response, from Monsieur George, is at the heart of the novel:
' "Inconstant", I whispered.' But in the face of his formulation, Leonore insists on restating her understanding, which
insists upon Rita's autonomy and her essential womanliness,
about which, she suggests, Monsieur George knows little.

This exchange suggests a source for much of the tension
that informs *The Arrow of Gold*, concerned as it is with
issues of legitimacy, sexual attraction, a woman's role in
politics, and a young man's coming to adulthood. At least
part of the search for maturity with which *An Arrow of Gold*
is concerned demands that Monsieur George come to know
himself as a man; in turn, that knowledge depends upon an
understanding of women. A series of men serve as tutors
and role models for George, but their inadequacy has much
to do with their inability to demonstrate a mature understanding of Rita through which George can come to his own
maturity in relation to her. Rita's maid attempts from time
to time to enlighten George, to remind him of her mistress's
humanity as he repeatedly tries to turn her into a polished
image.

' "Madame is not happy" ', the maid says simply to Monsieur George, who is as yet unable to appreciate such
directness and simplicity. For he tends always to turn Rita
into a metaphor or a symbol, preferring those to her simple
reality. So, on this occasion, he imagines her as a young
savage chieftain. Though she expresses herself in her usual
direct fashion, George persists in dehumanising her. Dis-

daining her quiet words, ' "I could hug you" ', the narrator explodes into a lengthy image which has the effect of mystifying Rita, turning her into a mysterious statue:

> She listened to me, unreadable, unmoved, narrowed eyes, closed lips, slightly flushed face, as if carved six thousand years ago in order to fix forever that something secret and obscure which is in all women. Not the gross immobility of a Sphinx proposing roadside riddles but the fiercer immobility, almost sacred, of a fateful figure seated at the very source of the passions that have moved men from the dawn of ages. (op. cit., p. 146)

This regular tendency to depersonalise Rita, to turn her into an image or a statue, characterises the behaviour of the narrator and the other men of the novel, in contrast to the women, who respond to Rita herself. Increasingly Rita reflects upon her isolation, her hopeless pursuit of genuine individuality. On the edge of tears she says to Monsieur George, ' "I don't know the truth about myself because I never had an opportunity to compare myself to anything in the world. I have been offered mock adulation, treated with mock reserve or with mock devotion. I have been fawned upon with an appalling earnestness of purpose, I can tell you" ' (op. cit., p. 207). It is interesting that just at the time of his life when *The Arrow of Gold* had been published, Conrad commented in what Najder describes as a 'surprisingly open letter' upon his own sense of isolation and misunderstanding:

> I have *la sensation du vide*. Not perhaps *le Vide Eternel*, though after sixty one may well begin to grow aware of it a little, but a certain inward emptiness. For 25 years I've been giving out all that was in me. But apart from that I have the feeling of approaching isolation. I don't say loneliness; I shall, I imagine, always be looked at now – but from a distance, as if set apart by my predestined temperament like some strange animal confined within a fence for public view. Through my fault – or is it simply Fate? – I have missed all along the chances of closer contacts.[7]

This extraordinary confidence, written to a virtual

stranger, suggests that with *The Arrow of Gold* Conrad confronted what had been a central concern of his artistic and personal life. For generations, critics have understood that this work was autobiographical, reflecting, in Monsieur George, the young Conrad's dangerous involvements in royalist politics. But with the last group of novels Conrad may well have found another kind of identification, as this letter suggests. In Rita's struggle for individuality and intimacy, we may read Conrad's own struggle which, towards the end of his life, he recognised as having essentially failed. For the ageing Conrad, reflecting in *The Arrow of Gold* upon his own youth, reflected as well upon his life experience, having become, in the eyes of even his closest friends, a kind of icon, regularly described in language which strikingly mirrors the language George uses to describe Rita. In the young Monsieur George Conrad explores the romance of his young life, while in Rita Conrad explores his paradoxical experience of lonely exoticism, of frustrated directness, marginal attractiveness. The loss of the mother, the absence of contemporary role models and mentors, the sense of alienation and difference are all Conrad's; at the same time, Monsieur George's tendency to turn Rita into a statue, an image false to her real self, is Conrad's as well. *The Arrow of Gold* might well be read as an intense musing about the connection between being a woman and being an artist, a subtext which is illuminated by Conrad's confidence to Warrington Dawson, who received his letter describing his loneliness.

It seems that over the years women characters came to represent aspects of Conrad's own experiences, the struggle to articulate a perception of reality, the desire to be understood for oneself, the attempt to achieve autonomy in a way that allowed for both intimacy and self-knowledge. At the same time, on a conscious level Conrad asserted his maleness, associating his artistry with his masculinity. Objecting to a French translation of *The Arrow of Gold* arranged by André Gide, he wrote indignantly: 'If my writings have a distinct character it lies in their virility – in their spirit and method of expression. No one has denied me that. And you throw me to women! One would think that you're taking me

for a fool.'[8] This alarm, as he objected to the hand of a
woman translator, suggests that *The Arrow of Gold* contains
something of significance to Conrad, since he had never
objected before to a woman's translation. Indeed, not long
afterwards he was comfortable assigning the translation of
Almayer's Folly to a Polish woman, authorising her to
choose her own equivalent expressions to correspond to his
idiomatic writing in English.[9] There must, then, be something particular about *The Arrow of Gold* for Conrad which
bears on his outburst at the prospect of this work being
translated by a woman who might rob him of his virility as
a writer.

A deep identification of the author with the central female
character might indeed explain Conrad's uneasiness and his
proprietary attitude towards the text. Ordinarily, critics
assume that the intention of *The Arrow of Gold* is to exalt
Rita from the particular to the general. As Daniel Schwartz
summarises, 'the novel dramatises George's futile attempts
to mythicise her and Conrad's folly in trying to transform
idiosyncrasies into archetypal qualities.'[10] However, the
suggestion that Conrad had come to identify himself with
the heroine whose subjectivity suffers from precisely the
objectifying which men attempt to impose upon it, presents
quite a different sort of achievement. Rita's expression of
despair at the regular mythologising she experiences is in
itself a powerful statement on the part of women characters
throughout the work of Conrad and other male writers.

What Rita sadly learns not to expect, even if not especially
from the men who claim to find her bewitching, is a form of
love which is founded on individuality and mutuality. For a
young man raised on sexual stereotypes and romance, such
as Monsieur George, Rita can only be an 'exotic' creature,
or a magnificent statue, not a particular, idiosyncratic
woman as subject. This tendency to romanticise, to see the
individual experience as the mythological, characterised
Conrad's earliest autobiographical heroes such as Marlow
in 'Youth' and *Heart of Darkness*. With age, the author came
to the creation of women characters who argued in their
lives and in their words against that generalising tendency.
Lena, in *Victory*, is only the most recent example before *The*

Arrow of Gold to resist that tendency to flatten individuality under a philosophical glaze. It is the nature of her struggle that she tries and fails to become uniquely real to Heyst, the abstracting and distancing son of the philosopher. The lesson that Heyst pronounces too late, to put one's trust in life, has everything to do with a recognition of that individuality and personal value which make reciprocal love possible between men and women.

George, a young man, commits the same injustice towards Rita that Heyst commits towards Lena: he regularly translates her individuality into an artistic stereotype, beautiful but unreal. Many critics have contended that Conrad was unable to create rounded characterisations of women, but it appears rather than Conrad's narrators are the ones who experience this difficulty. Reading past the narrator, the feminist reader regularly encounters women of distinct individuality. And it is often other women characters who direct the reader in the search for individuality and the expression of female singularity.

Rose, the young housemaid in *The Arrow of Gold*, regularly presents the narrator and the reader with evidence of thoughtful attention, understanding the needs and the feelings of her mistress while the narrator professes total bewilderment. ' "I am always on the watch" ', Rose says at one point, ' "but what is a poor girl to do?" ' (op. cit., p. 227) Her meaning for the reader is that, unlike the men who circle about Rita, a thoughtful and caring woman companion penetrates easily to the basic reality of Rita's situation: untroubled by the naïveté or the egotism that characterises Rita's male associates, women respond to Rita directly. The narrator excuses his apparent indifference to Rose's anxieties by reminding himself of his responsibilities. 'I had to appear insensible to her distress and that not altogether because, in fact, I had no option but to go away. I remember also a distinct willfulness in my attitude and something half contemptuous in my words as I laid my hand on the knob of the front door' (op. cit., p. 228). Like Marlow in *Chance*, the narrator of *The Arrow of Gold* takes refuge in the contemptuous tone to escape from the real need of a young woman in distress. In the case of Monsieur George, the representative of the young Conrad, there is a sense of his own incapacity, his unreadiness for the honest encounter that Rita represents. But there is also the realisation in the mature author that this unreadiness amounted to betrayal. For it is Rose, the maid, who hurls after him the real indictment of this text: ' "No! Madame has no friends. Not one!" ' (op. cit., p. 228).

In the concluding section of *The Arrow of Gold*, the issue of friendship pervades the text: the narrator, now the disembodied older male voice, speculates about the nature of the relationship between George and Rita. The narrator speculates, as well, about the effect upon the reader of such a relationship, such a narrative. He remarks: 'My conviction is that the mood in which the continuation of this story would appear sympathetic is very rare' (op. cit., p. 337). In fact, what he has to recount is a period of six months 'characterised more by a deep and joyous tenderness than by sheer passion.' In a paragraph filled with speculation about the nature of women's experience of love, the narrator at once exalts the nature of the love the two young people shared and dismisses it as having no interest for his readers. At the same time, the narrator seems determined to reserve for men the experience of total surrender of self to love, while confessing his lack of evidence for such an assertion. A desperate ambivalence characterises these pages, testifying perhaps to the uneasy relation between the author and his text. For in the end what distinguishes Rita is her honesty, a directness of self-revelation so great that no man can properly relate to it; so perfect a relation would demand a putting aside of egotism which proves impossible. Display and self-righteousness account for the resolution of the story, which culminates in a duel fought ostensibly on behalf of Rita's honour but in fact for the honour of her lover. Displaying himself perfectly unnecessarily, he invites recognition and himself issues the challenge which leads inevitably to his wound and Rita's departure from his life.

What will become of her? The answer given by the 'man of letters' is that 'she will be wasted' (op. cit., p. 350). This is finally the unambiguous dismissal which testifies to the depths of Conrad's understanding of the world he lived in and recreated. An exceptional woman, characterised from the first by intelligence and beauty, must be fated to be loved and misunderstood. Her recourse must finally be to disappear from the very world in which she was so capable, because men were made helpless and reckless by her presence in that world.

Conrad's last major work, *The Rescue*, takes up this issue of the capable, magnetic woman whose world exacts a frightful price for her abilities. Thomas Moser epitomises those critics who, encountering Edith Travers, react with that combination of condescension and anxiety which dismisses her pain while assigning responsibility for it to her. Moser writes: 'Mrs Travers has not really suffered. She has simply married a man who she thought was courageous and idealistic only to discover that he is the opposite.'[11] In the course of the novel, the nature and extent of Edith Travers's misfortune testify to the terrible constraints on a woman's opportunities for choice and development in a world which makes marriage the test of judgement and the only avenue of development. All the personal characteristics which make Edith Travers attractive to the reader and to the outsider, D'Alcacer or Tom Lingard, are the qualities which offend and disgust her husband, to whom she is irrevocably tied.

With *The Rescue*, Conrad returns from a new perspective to the confrontation between the world of Western civilisation and the world of Eastern native culture. In this novel the issue of women's development, women's need to be taken seriously as individuals, takes on new prominence. At the same time, the relations between women across cultural lines continue the line of exploration developed in *The Arrow of Gold*. The characteristics shunned by men of her own class serve to identify Edith Travers with the young native princess, Immada, reminding the reader that cultures differ in their willingness to accord power and stature to the capable woman: the price that Edith Travers pays for her quickness of mind and attractive body is not inevitable.

A young Captain Tom Lingard serves as the male protagonist in this novel, a man torn between his sense of responsibility to the natives who depend on him and his uneasy feeling of kinship with the white Westerners who call upon his racial loyalty. The strong appeal of Lingard and Edith Travers for one another clearly depends upon Lingard's relative freedom from the conventional standards applied to women within affluent Western culture. A voluntary exile from the West, Lingard has learned to value and to recognise the accomplishments of tribal women. Only too conscious of his own social deficiencies, he does not judge Edith Travers so much as he responds to her.

Thus Conrad returns in his maturity to the major theme of his earliest novels, those recognised as criticism of the imperialism which thrived on the achievements of men such as Tom Lingard. Choosing to depict Lingard in his younger days, at the end of his career Conrad provides a useful analysis of the ways in which Lingard became the tool of the class which condescends to him in *The Rescue*. By the time Lingard emerged in the first two novels, as a mature and over-confident Rajah Laut, he had mastered the ambiguity of his relation to his own culture and adopted the tone of the patriarch towards the natives who claim his allegiance and affection in *The Rescue*. What this late novel reveals is in large part how patriarchy creates its believers and demoralises its women.

It is clear in the novel, through its imagery and its characterisations, that the flower of civilisation, Edith Travers, suffers at the hands of those who profess love for her, while the flower of the native culture, Immada, radiates dignity and a sense of self-worth which are undeniable even to the cynical whites who observe her. With the casting off of her yachting outfit, and the donning of native women's clothing meant for the princess, Edith Travers provides a clear image of her desire for authenticity in the form of naturalness; her newly bared feet provide a particularly offensive provocation to her husband. ' "And you look simply heathenish in this costume" ', he points out, stung by her words but taking vengeance rather on her appearance. His gaze, she realises, is directed towards her feet, clad in native sandals. The deliberate conflation of clothing and attitude, the adoption of a direct and a natural tone by this woman of artifice and concealment, make clear to the reader the heady sense of freedom conferred by clothing appropriate to the climate (*The Rescue*, p. 275).

Critics have recognised the ways in which Edith Travers's perceptions and attitudes represent those of Conrad at this time of his life, though this recognition has not taken the form of an understanding that the book finishes a long-developing pattern. Daniel Schwartz perceives the connection between Edith Travers's powerful awareness of the darkness of the universe and Conrad's own pessimistic assessment of the moral world. But this sense of ominousness which Schwartz describes in cosmic terms[12] has much to do with the earlier issues of nature and culture, women and men. Edith Travers's despair comes directly from her personal and social condition, her unnatural and subservient relationship to a conventionally successful man whose intelligence does not match her own. Her vision of a lifetime of artifice and imprisonment, so coolly summed up and dismissed by Moser in his criticism of the novel, accounts for her apocalyptic vision of the night landscape. Schwartz's assertion that Edith Travers expresses Conrad's point of view suggests that close to the end of his writing career Conrad had arrived at some sense that he, as a writer and a perceptive analyst of Western culture, occupied the same ground as his thoughtful women characters. Karl notes that the style of *The Rescue* is actually quite unified, despite its having been worked on over a substantial number of years.[13] Since the early novels, focused on imperialism, depended upon their analysis through the eyes of critical women, this consistency of style and attitude in *The Rescue* seems a further indication of its incorporation of early insights.

The conclusions of *The Rescue* are almost entirely pessimistic. For Edith Travers, the return to the yacht and its voyage back to 'civilisation' promises a lifetime of artifice, disappointment and conventional relationships. Intelligent, untrained, chained to a wealthy bigot, she will retain her capacity for self-criticism and analysis but not the ability to change the confines of her life. For Lingard, there must also be self-criticism and self-doubt, a realisation that his loyalty to the whites who despised him cost the lives of the natives to whom he had become the 'Rajah Laut' they depended upon. The redeeming idea which was to justify imperialism, the vision of Western civilisation raising native aspirations, comes painfully to grief in *The Rescue*. A vision of natural, authentic behaviour, of relationships based on mutual honesty, falters as it did in *The Arrow of Gold*.

As in that novel so close to it in its time of creation, *The Rescue* suggests that women look to one another helplessly for understanding and support. Between Immada and Edith Travers there is a strong current of interest and curiosity, a sense of mutual admiration and longing for connection. Yet, as if responding to the strictures of Gayatri Chakravorty Spivak, Mrs Travers understands that in putting on the clothing of Immada she cannot ultimately do more than make it forever unavailable to Immada herself. In a passage of great subtlety, Conrad allows Edith Travers to experience the clothing and to reflect on the meaning of her use of it:

> No part of her costume made her feel so exotic [as the sandals]. It also forced her to alter her usual gait and move with short steps very much like Immada. 'I am robbing the girl of her clothes,' she had thought to herself, 'besides other things.' She knew by this time that a girl of such high rank would never dream of wearing clothing that had been worn by somebody else. (*The Rescue*, p. 285)

What Edith Travers understands is the futility of the disguise in which she has clothed herself, the attempt to put on, with the clothing, the innate dignity and sense of connection which inform Immada's bearing. 'She felt strongly her isolation', Conrad writes of Mrs Travers, an isolation expressed in terms of an empty landscape but representative of a social condition peculiar to a white woman of a particular class. Immada, like Nina Almayer and Aissa before her, expresses a natural connection to her tribe, her relations, and her own body. Edith Travers, on the contrary, comes to know that the presence of the yacht and the white people is 'fatal' to the culture which Immada and her brother represent and so naturally embody. ' "Is our presence here so

fatal?" ' Mrs Travers asks, only to be told, ' "It may be death
to some" ' (op. cit., p. 157). And of course it is the natives
who die, while the wealthy whites survive to continue their
lives of detached speculation.

Once again, as in *The Arrow of Gold*, the woman embodies
the capacity both to observe and to supply meaning to people
and events; like Rita de Lastaola, Edith Travers seems to
represent the artist at work:

> The occurrences of the afternoon had been strange in them-
> selves, but what struck her artistic sense was the vigour of their
> presentation. They outlined themselves before her memory with
> the clear simplicity of some immortal legend. They were mys-
> terious, but she felt they were absolutely true. They embodied
> artless and masterful feelings; such, no doubt, as had swayed
> mankind in the simplicity of its youth. She envied, for a
> moment, the lot of that humble and obscure sister. Nothing
> stood between that girl and the truth of her sensations. She
> could be sincerely courageous, and tender and passionate and –
> well, ferocious. (*The Rescue*, pp. 152–3)

Like the novelist, Edith Travers supplies meaning and
design to what she observes; and, like the novelist whose
creation she is, she laments the necessary formal distance
which separates her from the natural world. The ambiguous
nature of creation and the assignment of meaning comes in
these late novels to reside in the powerful women characters
who are at once subjects and observers of their own histories,
surrogates for the artist who wrestles with his responsibility
to the lives he tells.

In some ways, then, the novels of Conrad's last years
represent the fullest flowering of his investment in his
women characters. If it is true that they came to express
some of his own ambivalent sense of having turned into an
icon, a trapped observer of his own transformation, some of
the unease provoked by these books may be more easily
understood. The 'uncongenial subject' of romance between
men and women may not be solely responsible for the
critical responses these novels have long received, responses
which mingle belittling language with active dislike.

Women's marginality in the culture which pretends to

adore them, women's capacity for inwardness, for observation, and for a regular sense of being misunderstood
corresponds remarkably to the role of the artist as Conrad
envisioned and lived it. With the return to his early subject
matter in *The Rescue*, the shock of the encounter between
white and Malay cultures, Conrad brings together two major
preoccupations in a way which makes Edith Travers a particularly emblematic character. Woman as artist, woman as
marginal, woman as artefact, woman as recalcitrant and
articulate lover: all these Edith Travers represents, and in
all she embodies Conrad's own situation and history. As the
women in the early novels carried the moral weight, the
women in the late novels come to carry the shaping weight
of their novels.

> Thinking of what such life could be Mrs Travers felt invaded
> by that inexplicable exaltation which the consciousness of their
> physical capacities so often gives to intellectual beings. She
> glowed with a sudden persuasion that she also could be equal
> to such an existence; and her heart was dilated with a momen-
> tary longing to know the naked truth of things; the naked truth
> of life and passion buried under the growth of centuries. (op. cit.,
> p. 153)

With *The Rescue*, then, Conrad completes an investigative
line begun with his earliest works of fiction, taking his use
of women's voices and women characters to a new level of
meaning. Powerful and interesting in their own right, the
women of the late novels compel our attention as they come
closer to articulating the concerns of their author. Motherless, objectified, and deeply thoughtful, the women of the
late novels represent an advance in Conrad's work, rather
than the decline which is regularly attributed to them.

Conclusion

Joseph Conrad speaks to women, of women, throughout his work, at the deepest level. Fusing psychological and political concerns, Conrad regularly embodies his critical awareness of his art and his culture in the portraits of powerful women characters. Conrad understood, perhaps in part because of his own childhood experiences, the ways in which women may enter the culture differently from men and, in turn, be acted upon differently by the culture. He recognised the association between the imposition of the male will on the individual woman and the imposition of Western patriarchy on the native world of the Malay archipelago, the moral and sexual implications of an attitude of imperial conquest.

Later in his life, Conrad articulated as well the terrible sense of being misperceived and misunderstood which isolates women in their condition of marginality, muffles their voices, and confirms a bitter unreality. As Susan Lundvall Brodie notes, Conrad consciously uses female characters to suggest a particular 'artistic vision underlying the appearance of division and opposition'.[1] Female characters struggle for understanding in a world which makes their isolation palpable; in their marginal positions, they particularly long for the reassurance and reflection of other women. Especially in the late novels, Conrad focuses attention on that separation through narrative method (in *Chance*) and through imagery which emphasises the sense of imprisonment and misperception under which women struggle for autonomy and succeed infrequently, at terrible cost. No less pessimistic in his presentation of women than in his assessment of the condition of human existence, Conrad nevertheless regularly presents women in his later novels with the opportunity to affect relationships in irrevocable ways.

Although most critics agree that Conrad was least successful in his presentation of female characters, a close feminist analysis of his works demonstrates quite a different reality. Women characters engage the reader, reflect women's concerns and searches for solutions to social and political problems, and suggest alternative ways to describe and consider social reality. Women characters regularly confront the conditions of their lives in an integrated fashion. Unlike male characters who typically choose either the personal or the political means of expression, women characters typically work simultaneously in both spheres, effecting change on the psychic and the political levels at once. Conrad is unsentimental in his portrayals of even his most attractive women characters; despite their evident attachment to memories of his mother and past loves, the author struggles to provide for the women characters the authenticity and the recognition they call for in their texts.

In his thinking, Conrad was not a prisoner of his times; he was able to use his status as an outsider to retain that margin of critical thought which made his life uncomfortable and his readers often uneasy. Powerful women characters often experience and live out that uneasy consciousness, that sense of the perilous nature of material interests which are at the heart of Western culture. In our own times, when economic and cultural imperialism continue to be the expression of a patriarchy that is thousands of years old, we may do well to consider some of the insights which Conrad's women express in their impassioned criticism of their lives and their cultures, which are still very much our lives and cultures. The women in Conrad's life and in his texts have much to say to us.

Notes

INTRODUCTION

1. Bernard C. Meyer, MD, *Joseph Conrad: A psychoanalytical biography* (Princeton University Press, Princeton, NJ, 1967) p. 69.
2. Meyer, op. cit., p. 68.
3. Frederick R. Karl, *Joseph Conrad: The three lives. A biography.* (Farrar, Straus and Giroux, New York, 1979) p. 367.
4. Zdzislaw Najder, *Joseph Conrad: A chronicle* (Rutgers University Press, New Brunswick, NJ, 1983) p. xii.
5. Maggie Humm, *Feminist Criticism: Women as contemporary critics* (St. Martin's Press, New York, 1986) p. 69.
6. Humm, op. cit., p. 69.
7. Ruth Nadelhaft, 'Women as moral and political alternatives in Conrad's early novels', in Gabriela Mora and Karen S. Van Hooft, eds, *Theory and Practice of Feminist Literary Criticism* (Bilingual Press, Ypsilanti, Michigan, 1982) pp. 242–55.
8. Sherry B. Ortner, 'Is female to male as nature is to culture?', in Michelle Zimbalist Rosaldo and Louise Lamphere, eds, *Woman, Culture and Society* (Stanford University Press, Stanford, Calif., 1974).
9. Carolyn Merchant, *The Death of Nature: Women, ecology and the scientific revolution* (Harper and Row, New York, 1980) p. xv.
10. Merchant, op. cit., p. xvi.
11. Merchant, op. cit., p. 3.
12. Marianna Torgovnick, *Gone Primitive: Savage intellects, modern lives* (University of Chicago Press, Chicago, 1990) p. 156.

CHAPTER ONE

1. Susan Lundvall Brodie summarises such critical attitudes in her article, 'Conrad's feminine perspective', *Conradiana* Vol. 14, 1984, No. 2, p. 142.
2. Brodie, op. cit., p. 143.
3. Benita Parry, *Conrad and Imperialism: Ideological boundaries and visionary frontiers* (Macmillan, London, 1983) p. 16.
4. Stephen K. Land, *Conrad and the Paradox of Plot* (Macmillan, London, 1984) pp. 7–39.
5. Such critics as Jerry Allen and Norman Sherry traced Conrad's travels and tracked down records of people and places which served as the factual origins of the novels and tales.
6. Gayatri Chakravorty Spivak, 'Three women's texts', *Critical Inquiry*, Vol. 12, Autumn 1985. The argument works through the article.
7. Spivak, op. cit., p. 228.
8. Parry, op. cit., p. 3.
9. Parry, op. cit., p. 58.
10. Helen Funk Rieselbach, *Conrad's Rebels: The psychology of revolution from 'Nostromo' to 'Victory'* (UMI Research Press, Ann Arbor, Michigan, 1985) p. 8.
11. Daniel Schwartz, *Conrad: 'Almayer's Folly' to 'Under Western Eyes'* (Macmillan, London, 1980) p. 8.
12. Schwartz, op. cit., p. 10.
13. Frederick R. Karl, *Joseph Conrad: The three lives. A biography* (Farrar, Straus and Giroux, New York, 1979) p. 374.
14. Elaine Showalter, 'Shooting the Rapids: Feminist criticism in the mainstream', *Oxford Literary Review*, Vol. 8, 1986, p. 223.

CHAPTER TWO

1. Benita Parry, *Conrad and Imperialism: Ideological boundaries and visionary frontiers* (Macmillan, London, 1983) p. 12.
2. Thomas Moser, *Joseph Conrad: Achievement and decline* (Harvard University Press, Cambridge, Mass., 1957) p. 99.
3. Parry, op. cit., p. 64.
4. Sebastian Castellio, quoted in A. Ruth Fry's *Ruth's Gleanings: An anthology of prose and poetry* (Andrew Dakers Ltd, London, 1943) p. 32.
5. Marianna Torgovnick, *Gone Primitive: Savage intellects, modern lives* (University of Chicago Press, Chicago, 1990) p. 145.

6. Lillian Feder, 'Marlow's descent into hell', *Nineteenth-Century Fiction*, Vol. 9, 1955, p. 283.
7. Nina Auerbach, *Communities of Women: An idea in fiction* (Harvard University Press, Cambridge, Mass. and London, 1978) p. 84.
8. Auerbach, op. cit., p. 84.
9. Gayatri Chakravorty Spivak, 'Imperialism and sexual difference', *Oxford Literary Review*, Vol. 8, Nos. 1–2, 1986, p. 226.
10. Spivak, ibid.
11. Torgovnick, op. cit., p. 154.
12. Jacques Darras, *Joseph Conrad and the West: Signs of Empire* (Barnes and Noble, Totowa, NJ, 1982) p. 25.
13. Darras, op. cit., pp. 27–8.
14. Loúise Bernikow, ed., *World Split Open* (Viking, New York, 1974) Introduction, p. i.
15. Beverley Brown, ' "I read the metaphysic of morals and the categorical imperative and it doesn't help me a bit" ', *Oxford Literary Review*, Vol. 8, Nos. 1–2, 1986, p. 163.

CHAPTER THREE

1. Frederick R. Karl, *Joseph Conrad: The three lives. A biography* (Farrar, Straus and Giroux, New York, 1979) p. 546.
2. Karl, op. cit., p. 375.

CHAPTER FOUR

1. Zdzislaw Najder, *Conrad Under Familial Eyes* (Cambridge University Press, Cambridge, England, 1983b) pp. xiii–xiv.
2. Najder, op. cit., p. xv.
3. 'Ewa Korzeniowska to Apollo Korzeniowski, 10/22 May 1861', in Najder, *Conrad Under Familial Eyes*, p. 38.
4. 'Ewa Korzeniowska to Apollo Korzeniowski, 28 May/9 June 1861', in Najder, *Conrad Under Familial Eyes*, p. 44.
5. Najder, op. cit., p. xiv.
6. Claire Rosenfield, *Paradise of Snakes: An archetypal analysis of Conrad's political novels* (University of Chicago Press, Chicago, 1967) p. 60.
7. Helen Funk Rieselbach, *Conrad's Rebels: The psychology of revolution in the novels from 'Nostromo' to 'Victory'* (UMI Research Press, Ann Arbor, Michigan, 1985) p. 1.

8. Michael P. Jones, *Conrad's Heroism: A Paradise Lost* (UMI Research Press, Ann Arbor, Michigan, 1985) p. 122.
9. Carolyn G. Heilbrun, *Towards A Recognition of Androgyny* (Alfred A. Knopf, New York, 1973) p. 94.
10. Jocelyn Baines, *Joseph Conrad: A critical biography* (Weidenfeld and Nicolson, London, 1960) p. 337.
11. Baines, op. cit., pp. 337–8.
12. Baines, op. cit., p. 338.
13. Maureen Fries, 'Feminism–anti-feminism in *Under Western Eyes*', *Conradiana*, Vol. 5, 1973, pp. 63–4.
14. Daniel R. Schwartz, *Conrad: 'Almayer's Folly' to 'Under Western Eyes'* (Macmillan, London, 1980) p. 73.
15. Ewa Korzeniowska to Antoni Pietkiewicz, in Najder, *Conrad Under Familial Eyes*, p. 60.

CHAPTER FIVE

1. Helen Funk Rieselbach, *Conrad's Rebels: The psychology of revolution in the Novels from 'Nostromo' to 'Victory'* (UMI Research Press, Ann Arbor, Michigan, 1985) p. 87.
2. Daniel R. Schwartz, *Conrad: The later fiction* (Macmillan, London, 1982) p. 45.
3. Schwartz, op. cit., p. 46.
4. Schwartz, op. cit., p. 42.
5. Frederick R. Karl, *Joseph Conrad: The three lives. A biography* (Weidenfeld and Nicolson, London, 1960) p. 743.
6. Zdzislaw Najder, *Joseph Conrad: A chronicle* (Rutgers University Press, New Brunswick, NJ, 1983a) p. 409.
7. Najder, op. cit., p. 443.
8. Najder, op. cit., p. 447.
9. Najder, op cit. p. 450.
10. Schwartz, *Conrad: The later fiction*, p. 133.
11. Thomas Moser, *Joseph Conrad: Achievement and decline* (Harvard University Press, Cambridge, Mass., 1957) p. 104.
12. Schwartz, *Conrad: The later fiction*, pp. 121–3.
13. Karl, *Joseph Conrad: The Three Lives*, p. 816.

CONCLUSION

1. Susan Lundvall Brodie, 'Conrad's feminine perspective', *Conradiana* Vol. 14, 1984, No. 2, p. 141.

Select Bibliography

TEXTS

Conrad, Joseph, *Complete Works* (25 vols., Doubleday, Page & Company, New York, 1926). The dates of individual novels and stories are given in the text.

BIOGRAPHY

Baines, Jocelyn, *Joseph Conrad: A critical biography* (Weidenfeld and Nicolson, London, 1960).
Guerard, Albert, *Conrad the Novelist* (Harvard University Press, Cambridge, Mass., 1958).
Karl, Frederick R., *Joseph Conrad: The three lives. A biography* (Farrar, Straus and Giroux, New York, 1979).
Meyer, Bernard C., MD, *Joseph Conrad: A psychoanalytical biography* (Princeton University Press, Princeton, NJ, 1967).
Najder, Zdzislaw, *Joseph Conrad: A chronicle* (Rutgers University Press, New Brunswick, 1983a).
Najder, Zdzislaw, *Conrad Under Familial Eyes* (Cambridge University Press, Cambridge, 1983b).

CONRAD CRITICISM

Bradbrook, M. C., *Joseph Conrad: Poland's English genius* (Cambridge University Press, Cambridge, 1941).
Brodie, Susan Lundvall, 'Conrad's feminine perspective', *Conradiana* Vol. 14, 1984, No. 2, pp. 141–52.

Davidson, Arnold E., *Conrad's Endings: A study of the five major novels* (UMI Research Press, No. 39, Ann Arbor, Michigan, 1984).

Feder, Lillian, 'Marlow's descent into hell', *Nineteenth-Century Fiction*, Vol. 9, 1955, pp. 280–92.

Fries, Maureen, 'Feminism–anti-feminism in *Under Western Eyes*', *Conradiana*, Vol. 5, 1973, pp. 56–65.

Goodin, Richard, 'The personal and the political in *Under Western Eyes*', *Nineteenth-Century Fiction*, Vol. 25, 1970, pp. 327–42.

Hawkins, Hunt, 'The issue of racism in *Heart of Darkness*', *Conradiana*, Vol. 14, 1982, pp. 163–72.

Hay, Eloise Knapp, *The Political Novels of Joseph Conrad* (University of Chicago Press, Chicago, 1963).

Hunter, Allan, *Joseph Conrad and the Ethics of Darwinism: The challenge of science* (Croom Helm, London and Canberra, 1983).

Jones, Michael P., *Conrad's Heroism: A paradise lost*, Vol. 43 (UMI Research Press, Ann Arbor, Michigan, 1985).

Karl, Frederick R., *A Reader's Guide to Joseph Conrad* (Noonday Press, New York, 1960).

Martin, David M., 'The function of the Intended in Conrad's "Heart of Darkness"', *Studies in Short Fiction 11*, 1974, pp. 27–33.

Meyer, Bernard C., MD, 'The Agamemnon myth and *The Secret Agent*', *Conradiana*, Vol. 1, 1968, pp. 57–9.

Moser, Thomas, *Joseph Conrad: Achievement and decline* (Harvard University Press, Cambridge, Mass., 1957).

Parry, Benita, *Conrad and Imperialism: Ideological boundaries and visionary frontiers* (Macmillan, London, 1983).

Rieselbach, Helen Funk, *Conrad's Rebels: The psychology of revolution in the novels from 'Nostromo' to 'Victory'* (UMI Research Press, Ann Arbor, Michigan, 1985).

Rosenfield, Claire, *Paradise of Snakes: An archetypal analysis of Conrad's political novels* (University of Chicago Press, Chicago, 1967).

Schwartz, Daniel R., *Conrad: 'Almayer's Folly' to 'Under Western Eyes'* (Macmillan, London, 1980).

Schwartz, Daniel R., *Conrad: The later fiction* (Macmillan, London, 1982).

Watt, Ian, *Conrad in the Nineteenth Century* (University of California Press, Berkeley and Los Angeles, 1979).

GENERAL WORKS

Auerbach, Nina, *Communities of Women: An idea in fiction*

(Harvard University Press, Cambridge, Mass. and London, 1978).

Gilligan, Carol, *In a Different Voice: Psychological theory and women's development* (Harvard University Press, Cambridge, Mass. and London, 1982).

Greene, Gayle and Kahn, Coppelia, *Feminist Literary Criticism: Making a difference* (Methuen, London and New York, 1986).

Heilbrun, Carolyn G., *Towards a Recognition of Androgyny* (Alfred A. Knopf, New York, 1973).

Holland, Norman K., 'Transacting "My Good Morrow" or, bring back the vanishing critic', *Studies in the Literary Imagination*, Vol. XII, No. 1, Spring, 1979 (Georgia State University at Atlanta).

Humm, Maggie, *Feminist Criticism: Women as contemporary critics* (St. Martin's Press, New York, 1986).

Jacobus, Mary, *Reading Woman: Essays in feminist criticism* (Columbia University Press, New York, 1986).

Merchant, Carolyn, *The Death of Nature: Women, ecology and the scientific revolution* (Harper and Row, New York, 1980).

Showalter, Elaine, 'Shooting the Rapids: Feminist criticism in the mainstream', *Oxford Literary Review*, Vol. 8, 1986.

Spivak, Gayatri Chakravorty, 'Three women's texts and a critique of imperialism', *Critical Inquiry*, Vol. 12, Autumn, 1985.

Spivak, Gayatri Chakravorty, 'Imperialism and sexual difference', *Oxford Literary Review*, Vol. 8, 1986.

Torgovnick, Marianna, *Gone Primitive: Savage intellects, modern lives* (University of Chicago Press, Chicago, 1990).

Index